LIZZIE BORDEN
TOOK AN AXE, OR DID SHE?

LIZZIE BORDEN
TOOK AN AXE, OR DID SHE?

A Rhetorical Inquiry

Annette M. Holba

<teneo> // press

YOUNGSTOWN, NEW YORK

ISBN: 978-1-934844-01-4

This book is dedicated to my mom,
Elizabeth June Umberger,
who passed away as I finished this manuscript

I miss you

… love you, Mom.

Lizzie Borden took an axe
And gave her mother forty whacks
When she saw what she had done
She gave her father forty-one

TABLE OF CONTENTS

ACKNOWLEDGMENTS

This is a project that has been in the making since my adjunct teaching years at Rutgers University, Camden, NJ, where I taught Victimology in the Criminal Justice Department and at Rowan University, Glassboro, NJ, where I taught Women and Crime. As a former prosecutor's detective and as an adjunct in these Criminal Justice Departments, I became interested in the case of Lizzie Borden out of sheer mystery and wonderment. As I changed careers and moved into the academy by earning a Ph.D. in Rhetoric at Duquesne University, the case of Lizzie Borden has never left my mind. In my current position at Plymouth State University, I developed a first-year seminar course entitled, *Lizzie Borden Took an Axe, Or Did She?* in which we explore the case and develop critical thinking skills by analyzing various mediated artifacts that represent the Borden story. Because there are a plethora of media offerings related to Lizzie Borden's case, I feel it can be a popular culture case study that can help new college students to develop critical thinking skills while introducing them to theories of human communication in a context that is interesting and potentially familiar to them. My interest (or as some suggest, obsession) in this case will probably not wane soon.

Over the course of the last several years, I have had the opportunity to publish my Lizzie Borden work to a community of Borden enthusiasts through the (former) *Lizzie Borden Quarterly* and the scholarly magazine, *The Hatchet: Journal of Lizzie Borden Studies*, Stefani Koorey, Editor. Stefani has been extremely supportive in cultivating my interests in publishing about Lizzie and extremely helpful with her excellent editing and writing skills in assisting me to lose some of my scholarly jargon and write about Lizzie for an audience removed from any pretenses—people who share my interest and passion about the case of Lizzie Borden from all walks of life. Stefani, while we haven't met, you are dear to me and I thank you for everything.

To my husband, Dan, who put up with my late nights of writing to finish this project. For me, Lizzie Borden's case will never rest and Dan understands this—thank you. For Emily, a Springer Spaniel who has learned about things ranging from Plato to Lizzie—you are a true and patient friend. To Michele and Christina, thank you for your patience as I talked your ear off about Lizzie adventures. To Christina, thank you for your steadfast effort at reading and editing the final pages of this manuscript. To my dad, Bill, you are a great inspiration to me, and to my mom, June, who passed away as I completed this manuscript, thank you for your support as I eagerly shared my ideas about Lizzie with you...I miss you. To my mother-in-law, Shirley, you are simply fantastic! To the rest of my family—all of you—thank you for your support and tolerance of my ideas. Dr. Richard Thames, thank you for patiently helping me to understand a little bit more about doing rhetorical criticism and supporting my Lizzie passion! It is with deep appreciation and gratitude that I thank Pat Arneson for her help. Pat is a dear and diligent friend who has intellectual generosity and a never-ending drive to cultivate ideas. I thank you from the bottom of my heart, *verbum sat sapienti*. I also want to thank all the editors from Teneo Press who has been gracious with me through this whole process. Finally, thank you, Lizbeth Borden, for the legacy you left to us—may you rest in peace.

INTRODUCTION

As we consider the past we can learn about human nature and forge changes in our future. The failure to critically explore and consider implications of past actions may consequently create false notions that manifest into legends and myths that impose a truth far removed from actual lived experience. It is through this ignorance that people are misled. That is why I chose to explore issues surrounding the myth/legend of the infamous Lizzie Andrew Borden. A myth is a popular belief that has evolved over time around something or someone that embodies a particular ideal or set of ideals situated in a public space within society—this myth is often exaggerated or sometimes totally false. Following along this same thought, a legend can be considered a story of sorts that has been passed down through generations or a tradition about a person, place, or thing. The story is often exaggerated and open to interpretation or it is intentionally misrepresented. A significant implication of myth and legend is that misinformation creates a false impression and misunderstanding, which is not particularly helpful if we want to learn from our past.

Lizzie Borden is infamous because of the passing down of false information, rumors, speculation, and exaggeration. This false information, which originated at the time Lizzie's father and stepmother were murdered in their own home, was perverted through rumors and misconceptions of Lizzie's presumed guilt. As information passes through generations of changing historical moments, misconceptions help to develop the legendary and the mythical Lizzie Borden. One example of this, from a personal perspective, is the fact that I always thought that Lizzie Borden was a young teenaged child when she hacked to death her parents. I recall playing with friends, as a young child, jumping rope and singing:

> *Lizzie Borden took an axe*
> *And gave her mother forty whacks*
> *And when she saw what she had done*
> *She gave her father forty-one*

The impression that I remember is that Lizzie was a young girl of about the age of thirteen or fourteen years. I was afraid of the little girl who did the unthinkable…*kill her parents with an axe*. I envisioned this *girl* taking an axe that one might chop wood with and viciously attacking her parents. I never knew that they both were not her biological parents. I never knew that Lizzie was thirty-two at the time she was accused of committing this crime. I never knew she had been *acquitted* of the crime. Through my own investigation into the Lizzie Borden narrative, my impression of the Lizzie Borden story today is radically different than when I first began my inquiry.

There are two main questions that we must consider before moving forward with this book. First, what is rhetorical inquiry and second, how does rhetorical inquiry provide valuable insight into how we might comprehend the incomprehensible? By answering these two questions we help to situate a textured understanding of rhetoric within our everyday experience and allow it to guide our critical thinking abilities. We'll learn about theories of human communication. We'll learn about rhetorical inquiry. We'll learn about asking different questions. We'll learn about cultivating critical thinking through issues, reasons, reasoning, identifying fallacies, communicative ambiguity, assumptions, evidences, omissions, and interpretive possibilities. This text includes five essays previously published in either the *Lizzie Borden Quarterly* or *The Hatchet: Journal of Lizzie Borden Studies* to bring together rhetorical insight and new ways of understanding the historical artifacts that created the legend and myth of Lizzie Borden. This text invites the reader to think outside of the box in a way that is sometimes limited through our mediated world. Let's begin by considering the first question—what is rhetorical inquiry?

RHETORICAL INQUIRY

Rhetorical inquiry allows one to gain a perspective about real events that can sometimes be distorted by opinion, rumor, gossip, and those things we refer to as factoids, which are based upon a real event but far removed from the truth. Aristotle (1984) defined rhetoric as "the faculty of observing in any given case the available means of persuasion" (p. 24). Adopting Aristotle's definition of rhetoric, we are able to see how rhetorical inquiry has a persuasive component. When we approach an investigation, an inquiry, or an interpretation of particular events, we encounter and we are confronted by persuasion. In this encounter and confrontation a discovery emerges and our knowledge of a particular event becomes textured. Communication scholars in the mid-twentieth century suggested that rhetoric is to be informative and suasory discourse (Bryant, 1953). Rhetoric, in this sense, is identified as being in a contingent category rather than an objectively scientific category. Rhetoric has also been described as a system of rhetorics rather than a singular concept (Ehninger, 1968). Other scholars expand the definition of rhetoric from this Aristotelian conceptualization focused on persuasion to include other outcomes, such as, to achieve clarity through the use of symbols, the notion of a semiotic aesthetic awakening, or the act of carefully developing mutual understanding through the use of symbols (Herrick, 2005). It is clear in this case that the image—the symbolic representation, is paramount in the understanding of rhetoric in every day experience.

Rhetoric as a system of inquiry can be described similarly as Burghardt (2000) describes rhetorical criticism. According to Carl Burchardt, rhetorical criticism is focused on assessing persuasive appeals and effects of public oratory in a context. Rhetorical inquiry, then, is a mode of evaluating the persuasive appeals and effects of public discourse, artifacts, and situated utterances in a methodical fashion. The outcome of rhetorical inquiry involves the development of an intellectual history of a given situation or context. Add to this notion the idea of inquiry as a routine and explicit conversation (Rorty, 1979), and we have a better understanding of how this rhetorical look at Lizzie Borden is approached. In this very public conversation or inquiry, this book seeks to expand the intellectual history of the case surrounding Lizzie Borden by assessing the persuasive appeals and effects of these appeals of public discourse, artifacts, and situated utterances embedded within the Lizzie Borden narrative.

VALUABLE INSIGHT

How does rhetorical inquiry provide valuable insight to our comprehension of the incomprehensible? In this case, the real-life experience of Lizzie Borden, who was accused of using an axe to kill her father and stepmother, offers a unique opportunity for us to gain new knowledge. Part of this rhetorical inquiry involves looking at several communication and rhetorical theories of human communication. Sometimes theories can be presented far removed from lived action, which can make our understanding less appealing, less connected to reality, and more abstract in general. Theory offers valuable insight into motive, historical moments, narrative connections, and many other theoretical underpinnings that open insightful direction for our understanding and comprehension. Theoretical perspectives offer multiple ways of interpretation that enhance understanding without setting boundaries or limits upon one's interpretation. In this way the ability to critically analyze, interpret, synthesize, and evaluate a given situation helps us to be better critical thinkers and better ethical human agents.

What makes this text particularly noteworthy? I can respond to this question in two ways. My first response is that communication theory is often disconnected from the lived experience or it is considered in such an abstract way that applying concepts or predicting communicative behavior is difficult. This text has taken a few select communication theories and demonstrated their interpretive potential applied within a real world context which can help us develop critical thinking skills that we can apply in other contexts. My second response is that I use a popular culture artifact, the case of Lizzie Borden, because it has relevancy to us today in that it resonates with similar contemporary cases, so we can learn from this inquiry and use a similar approach(es) to understand these contemporary cases. Thanks to CNN and other 24-hour news offerings, people today have access to news stories 24 hours a day from all around the world. Being a better critical thinker simply makes us savvy to what is happening around us at any given moment. The case of Lizzie Borden is familiar to many and imbued with mystery so that our interest is peaked and maintained. Additionally, the case of Lizzie Borden is not the first case of parricide, or patricide for that matter, in history. In fact, in our recent popular culture consciousness there have been several cases of parricide that have gained national attention in the United States. For example, on November 13, 1974, Ronald Defeo killed his mother, father, and siblings; he is serving a life sentence in a New York State prison (thus, setting the stage for the popular culture phenomenon *The Amityville Horror*); on August 20, 1989, brothers Lyle and Erik Menendez killed their parents for their inheritance; they are each serving a life sentence in different prisons in California; on November 15, 2006, Christopher Porco killed his father and attempted to kill his mother; he was convicted and is serving a twenty-five year to life sentence in a New York State prison, mandating he had to serve a minimum of fifty years before consideration for parole. There are many more cases of parricide[1] (matricide, patricide, infanticide) in our everyday media exposure. This makes the case of Lizzie Borden also relevant to consumers within popular culture. The hope of this text is to consider the case of Lizzie Borden from a scholarly perspective that will demonstrate its ability to teach us critical thinking skills and help us to apply communication/rhetorical theory to lived action, and enjoy the experience.

OVERVIEW OF CHAPTERS

Before moving forward with this rhetorical inquiry, an overview of the chapters and the theories that will guide our journey is necessary. Chapter 1, *Emplotment: The Cast, The Facts, The Story*, begins with a synopsis of the case of Lizzie Borden. Here the facts of the case are presented so that readers have an understanding of the facts as opposed to opinion and rumor that are responsible for distorting the circumstances. Chapter 2, *Lizzie Borden: A Rhetorical Inquiry*, considers the rhetorical aspects of scapegoat, mystery, propaganda, and dramatism as posited by rhetorical theorist Kenneth Burke. Chapter 3, *Lizzie Borden, Media, and Historicity*,

---

[1] "Patricide" is a subcategory of "parricide"—the murdering of one's father. Parricide refers to one who commits the act of murdering a close relative. For the purpose of this text I use "parricide" because Lizzie Borden was charged with the murders of Andrew and Abby Borden, father and stepmother.

hermeneutically examines media and historicity through Edwin Porter's *A Fall River Tragedy*. In this chapter historicity, historical consciousness, and historically-effected consciousness are explored in Porter's mediated account at the time the investigation and trial was occurring. By using Hans-Georg Gadamer's philosophical hermeneutics and Paul Ricoeur's narrative within the historically-effected consciousness, recuperation of Porter's misrepresentations can be accomplished. Chapter 4, *From Lizzie to Lizbeth: What's in a Name?*, is an examination of Lizzie's name change from Lizzie Andrew Borden to Lizbeth Borden and considered through Kenneth Burke's notion of purge and catharsis, Richard Weaver's linguistic covenant, and Michael Hyde's linguistic acknowledgment. What are the rhetorical implications of a name? We'll consider the possibilities in this chapter. Chapter 5, *Forensic Analysis and Rhetorical Discrepancies*, explores official testimony of various witnesses as well as including an essay entitled, "The Trial Testimony of John V. Morse" previously published in *The Hatchet: Journal of Lizzie Borden Studies* that explores the trial testimony of Morse specifically. This analysis identifies points of stasis in forensic oratory that can be analyzed through Cicero's stasis invention method. This chapter challenges what (we think) we know and asks us to consider other possibilities. Chapter 6, *The Lizzie Borden Narrative*, explores the Borden narrative through Walter Fisher's narrative paradigm (which was also addressed in chapter 5) but is extended through the work of Kathleen Glenister Roberts who textures the narrative paradigm with the performance paradigm for enriched understanding and comprehension of how narratives situate meaning. This chapter considers the terms "story" and "narrative" and asks the question, "Is there a Lizzie narrative?" The case specific aspect to be considered in this chapter is the rhetorical narrative of gender bias and the ongoing dialectic at the time of the murders. Chapter 7, *After all These Years*, asks the question, "So what?" Why are we still interested in a case that is over one hundred years old when there have been interesting and unique criminal cases since then? The answer is simply that there are multiple ways to negotiate interpretations of this matter that have not yet been fully realized. We are interested in Lizzie Borden's experiences because of the mystery and because there are interpretive possibilities that resonate with our own historical moment. The selected essay in this case involves a consideration of sexual orientation, a relevant topic in the public forum today—but not one hundred years ago. So, there are new ways to interpret based upon our own historical moment. This case is historically significant to the criminal justice system in general, to women's issues, and it is certainly better situated for valuable discussion in a postmodern era that has moved beyond a postmodern shock of uncertainty and into a postmodern beyondness (Holba, 2007) that invites multiple voices to participate in the conversation—at least theoretically. And last but not least—the most significant rhetorical contribution of the case in point:

> *Lizzie Borden took an axe*
> *And gave her mother forty whacks*
> *When she saw what she had done*
> *She gave her father forty-one*

This little ditty acts as a rhetorical trope that will undoubtedly stand within our memories for our lifetime. Chapter 8 offers brief concluding remarks. Let us begin our journey into the case of Lizzie Borden and use it as a rhetorical nudge to help us better understand and apply communication theories and teach us to be better critical thinkers.

References

Aristotle. (1984). *The rhetoric.* New York: Modern Library College Editions.

Bryant, D. C. (1953). Rhetoric: Its function and scope. *Quarterly Journal of Speech.* 39, 401–424.

Burgchardt, C. R. (Ed.) *Readings in rhetorical criticism.* State College, PA: Strata Publishing.

Ehninger, D. (1968). On the systems of rhetoric. *Philosophy and Rhetoric.* 1, 131–144.

Herrick, J. A. (2005). *The history and theory of rhetoric: An introduction.* Boston: Allyn and Bacon.

Holba, A. (2007). *Philosophical leisure*: *Recuperative praxis for human communication.* Milwaukee, WI: Marquette University Press.

Rorty, R. (1979). *Philosophy and the mirror of nature.* Princeton, NJ: Princeton University Press.

LIZZIE BORDEN
TOOK AN AXE, OR DID SHE?

CHAPTER 1

EMPLOTMENT:
THE CAST, THE FACTS, THE STORY

ANDREW JACKSON BORDEN was sixty-nine years old at the time of his death (Rebello, 1999). He was one of the wealthiest individuals in Fall River at the time. Andrew Borden was the president of one of the larger banks in Fall River and held high positions in other banks. Borden had several real estate holdings and engaged in business ventures with other wealthy businessmen. He was married twice. Historians suggest that Andrew Borden, although he came from a line of Bordens that were once the wealthiest family, had lost some of the once owned wealth and vowed to reclaim what his forefathers had claimed (Brown, 1992). Andrew Borden made money any way that he could, but he did not spend it in a manner that was "fashionable" and he did not demonstrate, borrowing a couplet from Thorstein Veblen (1899/1960), "conspicuous consumption" (p. 60)—rather he was thrifty and tight with his money.

The Bordens did not have running hot water in the home, their house was not connected to gas lines that would have brought lights into their home, and the Borden home did not have a telephone line connected to the house. Andrew Borden saw no use for the added expense for these luxuries. Whether or not Andrew Borden had a will is somewhat a mystery, but we can now consider some inferences. There are several possibilities concerning the existence of a will (or not): either he did and it was never found, or he did and Andrew Jennings, his family lawyer and Lizzie's defense attorney, never turned it over. Another possibility would be that he felt no need for it, just like he felt no need for gas, running water, or telephone lines to his house.

Andrew Borden's first wife was SARAH MORSE BORDEN. Together they had two children that survived, Emma Lenora Borden, born March 1, 1851, and Lizzie Andrew Borden, born July 19, 1860. Prior to the birth of Lizzie, Sarah gave birth to another female child who did not survive. In March of 1863 Sarah Borden died of "uterine congestion" and a "disease of the spine" (Rebello, 1999, p. 6) and at the time, Lizzie was almost three years old. Lizzie would later recount during her inquest testimony that she regarded Emma as her mother figure instead of her stepmother, Abby Durfee Borden, Andrew's second wife. Andrew Borden did not marry Abby Durfee until 1865, two years after the death of Sarah. During those two years Lizzie learned to rely upon Emma for the nurturing that a mother would normally provide.

ABBY DURFEE GRAY BORDEN married Andrew Borden in 1865 when she was thirty-seven years old. Abby was from another wealthy family in the area, and she was described as a large woman. It has been speculated that Andrew, knowing he needed a mother figure for his daughters and someone to maintain the household, married out of need rather than love. Andrew and Abby never had a child of their own. Abby's household responsibilities included caring for Emma and Lizzie and cleaning the second floor bedrooms. The rest of the home was maintained by Bridget, the maid at the time of the murders.

EMMA LENORA BORDEN was born on March 1, 1851 to Andrew and Sarah Borden. As mentioned previously, Emma, being the oldest daughter, took over much of the responsibility of caring for Lizzie when Sarah, their mother, died. Emma did not have a good relationship with Abby Borden, and she often made herself scarce when she was old enough to leave the Borden house unaccompanied. Emma kept a bedroom at the Borden residence but often did not stay there once she could travel on her own. Shortly before the murders of Andrew and Abby Borden, Emma switched bedrooms with Lizzie, taking the smaller bedroom while giving the larger bedroom to Lizzie. At the time of Andrew and Abby's murders, Emma was visiting friends out of the area.

LIZZIE ANDREW BORDEN was born July 19, 1860. She was the third birth of Sarah Borden; the second child died at birth about two years prior to Lizzie's birth. Lizzie was not quite three years old when her mother died. Two years later when Andrew remarried Abby Durfee Borden, Lizzie had difficulty adjusting to her new mother figure because she learned to rely on Emma for everything and she may have also felt the special bond she had with her father would now be threatened by this new intruder into the Borden home. Lizzie never considered Abby her *mother* and made quite sure that everyone knew this. It is not clearly known if Lizzie was actively or seriously involved with any suitors. She was actively involved in her church and with the Women's Christian Temperance Union. At the time of her death, she bequeathed thirty thousand dollars to the Society for the Protection of Animals. To describe Lizzie's physical appearance, at the time of the murders she was thirty-two years old, attractive, average weight for her petite height, and she always maintained a most "proper" appearance.

JOHN VINNICUM MORSE was Andrew Borden's brother-in-law from his first marriage. Morse was the brother of Sarah Morse Borden. Little is ever told of Morse other than he engaged in business ventures with Andrew, and he stayed in touch with Andrew Borden after Sarah's death. The evening prior to the murders, Morse arrived at the Borden residence to stay for a few days. It is unknown if this was a planned visit, although he had visited the Borden home on occasion after his sister's death. In this particular visit, Morse did not bring a travel bag with him. Lizzie was out during the evening when he arrived. When she returned home she went up the rear stairs directly to her room. Lizzie testified that she knew he was there because she heard him speaking to Andrew but never went to greet him. Lizzie also testified at the inquest that she heard raised voices between her father and her uncle but she was unable to decipher what they were "talking" about.

BRIDGET SULLIVAN was the Borden family maid. The Bordens had recently gone through several maids and, in this case in particular, there was another servant who may have been very close to Emma and Lizzie, and her name was Maggie. The name "Maggie" seemed to attach itself to every servant after Maggie left the Borden employment. Bridget Sullivan was a trustworthy and hard-working servant. At the time of the murders, Bridget was home, at the Borden residence, cleaning windows and resting in her third floor attic bedroom afterward.

ANDREW JENNINGS was not only Lizzie's defense counsel but also Andrew's family and business attorney. Andrew Jennings never discussed this case after Lizzie's acquittal. Jennings would most likely be the only other person to know whether or not Andrew had prepared a will.

HONORABLE A. E. PILLSBURY was the Attorney General of Massachusetts at the time of the Borden murders. Pillsbury and District Attorney Knowlton corresponded with each other about the fact that there was no real evidence to take this matter of Lizzie as the suspect to trial but that due to public rage created by the media, they had no choice other than to formally take her through the system.

HOSEA KNOWLTON was the District Attorney at the time of these murders. At times Knowlton demonstrated frustration with the case as he pursued an aggressive line of questioning in order to get Lizzie to "confess." As previously mentioned, Knowlton discussed media influence with Attorney General Pillsbury because he felt it was the public pressure driving the criminal pursuit and not the hard evidence of the case.

RUFUS HILLIARD was in charge of the police investigation that has been described as sloppy or short-sighted. Some critics compare the Fall River police investigation (at the time of the murders) to the comedic images of bumbling Keystone cops. The fact is, Fall River police had virtually no experiences with cases of this magnitude and certainly no training focused on these types of cases.

DR. WILLIAM DOLAN was the Medical Examiner. He was not the first medical doctor on the scene, but he conducted the postmortem examinations that would become significant to determining time of death and other forensic analyses.

DR. SEABURY BOWEN was the family doctor who resided across the street. He was the first medical doctor on the scene. Surprisingly, Bowen testified as an expert at the inquest, but by the time of the trial, he tried to minimize his testimony. Bowen has been identified as a significant "player" in one of the most provocative theories presented by Arnold Brown (1992) that suggests Bowen changed his testimony and burned possible evidence in the family stove.

HONORABLE JOSIAH BLAISDELL was the judge who presided over the inquest and preliminary hearing. While the defense argued that

Blaisdell would be biased if he presided over the preliminary hearing due to his involvement with the inquest, Blaisdell declined to recuse himself and continued to preside over the preliminary hearing. At the end of the preliminary hearing, Blaisdell ordered that Lizzie Andrew Borden was "probably guilty" and the case was forwarded to the grand jury for review and indictment (true bill). Any possible jury member who may have heard this charge of "probably guilty" would undoubtedly be influenced.

ADELAIDE CHURCHILL lived next door to the Borden residence. Their side yards were very close. Lizzie saw Mrs. Churchill while looking out her side door and called for Churchill to come over to her house. Lizzie yelled out to her that someone had killed her father. Churchill was a very important witness because she saw Lizzie shortly after Andrew was murdered, and she could testify as to Lizzie's demeanor as well as her physical appearance. In Brown's (1992) theory that involves Dr. Bowen, Mrs. Churchill becomes important in that she could testify as to whether or not Dr. Bowen was alone with Lizzie prior to arrival of police officials.

ALICE RUSSELL was Lizzie's best friend at the time. Lizzie visited Alice the evening before the murders. Lizzie confided in Alice that she feared something bad was going to happen in her home. Lizzie explained that she had seen strangers lurking around the house and that the house had been broken into in the recent past. Lizzie also confided in Russell that Andrew was having trouble with someone over a business issue and it scared her. Alice Russell's grand jury testimony was significant in that without it, Lizzie may not have been indicted. In fact, the grand jury was adjourned for several days prior to Russell coming forward with the story that she saw Lizzie burn a dress a few days after the murders. Until then, the police had no evidence to directly link Lizzie to the crime (and not that this story offers direct evidence either), nevertheless, after this testimony, Lizzie was indicted for the murders of her father and stepmother.

ELI BENCE was a druggist who reported that he believed Lizzie Borden attempted to purchase prussic acid, a type of poison used for cleaning particular materials, several days prior to the crime. However, after all the media attention, hype, and conjecture about a poison motive, 1) Bence was unable to identify Lizzie as the woman who tried to purchase prussic acid beyond a reasonable doubt, 2) the alleged attempt to purchase the acid occurred too remote in time from the actual crime, and 3) the method, poison, is not consistent with the actual mode of murder, being blunt force trauma, so his testimony was never used at the trial.

HANNAH REGAN was a jail matron and was part of a scam when she lied and stated that she heard a conversation between Emma and Lizzie while Lizzie was incarcerated. The conversation indicated that Lizzie was concerned that Emma would give her up. Later the story was revealed as a hoax.

RECALLING THE CASE OF LIZZIE BORDEN

The facts of this case are simply that on August 4, 1892, two people were murdered in their home at 92 Second Street, Fall River, Massachusetts. The victims were Andrew Jackson Borden and his second wife, Abby Durfee Gray Borden. There were two other household members in the immediate area that morning—Lizzie Borden, Andrew's daughter from his first marriage, and the maid, Bridget Sullivan (nicknamed Maggie). Lizzie Borden found her father and called to Bridget who was resting in her bedroom located on the third floor of the residence. Lizzie called to Bridget from the parlor where she found her father's body.

Sources vary on the actual number of wounds to each victim, indicating that Abby Borden received approximately eighteen to twenty-one wounds to her head and neck area while Andrew Borden received nine to eleven to his head and neck area. The investigation at the time determined through an analysis of stomach contents and analysis of blood surrounding the wounds that Abby Borden was murdered approximately an hour and a half prior to her husband. While this fact is now being disputed by William Masterton (2000) who wrote *Lizzie didn't do it!*, we can still legitimately conclude that Abby Borden was killed prior to Andrew Borden's murder.

It is fact that Emma Borden, sister of Lizzie, was away visiting friends that week. It is also true that the evening prior to the murders, John Morse had arrived for a visit.

Lizzie Borden was the first and last suspect in this investigation. The investigation has not been officially reopened in an attempt to solve the murders. There were four legal proceedings: the inquest, preliminary hearing, grand jury, and the trial. The murders were committed on August 4, 1892 and by June 20, 1893, Lizzie Andrew Borden had been tried and acquitted of the murders. During the ten months that transpired between the murders and the trial there were rumors, lies, innuendos, and an advancing assault on the character of Lizzie Borden. These facts are indisputable. As the information expanded to conflicting testimony and faulty memories, any potential truth became distorted. Let's now place these murders into a context.

THE MURDERS

August 4, 1892 started out as a typical warm summer day in Fall River, Massachusetts. The Borden family, Andrew, Abby, Lizzie, and Emma lived at 92 Second Street with their maid, Bridget Sullivan. On this particular day Emma was not home; in fact, she had been out of town visiting friends. Andrew, Abby, and Lizzie all felt ill for a few days prior to the day of the murders. Lizzie visited her friend, Alice Russell, the night before the murders. Lizzie confided in Alice that she believed there was potential danger about to fall upon the Borden home. Lizzie had concerns over some business associates of her father. Lizzie's uncle, John Morse, arrived at the Borden home on August 3rd and planned to stay overnight. Lizzie would later testify that when she arrived home from her visit with Alice, she went straight to her room without entering the parlor and without acknowledging her father, Andrew, or her uncle, John Morse. Lizzie would later testify at the inquest that as she lay in her bed for the night she would hear their angry raised voices. She knew her father and uncle were arguing, but she could not make out the nature of the disagreement.

According to inquest testimony, the next morning Lizzie remained in her room until her uncle left for the day. Andrew Borden left the residence after John Morse. When Lizzie descended the stairs she conversed with the maid, Bridget, and her stepmother, Abby. Abby asked Lizzie what she wanted for dinner but Lizzie indicated she did not feel well. Testimony after this point in time becomes inconsistent and corroboration is difficult. Lizzie claimed Abby told her a note came from a sick friend and she would be leaving to go visit the friend. Lizzie never inquired further about the note. Sometime around 9:30 a.m., Abby was murdered while making the bed in the guestroom where Morse slept the night before. Sometime after 10:30 a.m., Andrew returned home early carrying a white parcel in his hand. The door was locked on the inside and Bridget had to unbolt it. Bridget had just finished cleaning windows, as instructed by Abby after Andrew Borden and Morse left earlier that morning. Lizzie met her father in the parlor, exchanged some words with him and helped him get comfortable on the sofa. Then she left the room and went to the barn to look for lead sinkers for an upcoming fishing trip.

Just prior to 11:00 a.m., Bridget stopped her chores and went to her third floor bedroom in the attic to rest for a while because she felt sick. A few minutes after 11:00 a.m., Lizzie returned from the barn and found her father dead on the sofa in the parlor. She called out to Bridget to get a doctor. In the confusion, Bridget ran for Dr. Bowen at his residence across the street but he wasn't home. At Lizzie's instruction, she then ran for a friend, Alice Russell. While Lizzie waited for someone to return, a neighbor, Mrs. Churchill, saw her at the side door. Lizzie called out to Mrs. Churchill that someone had killed her father. It wasn't until later that when asked where her stepmother might be, Lizzie indicated she had gone out but that she might have returned. Bridget and Mrs. Churchill ascended the front stairs to find Abby Borden dead in the guestroom. From this point on newspaper reporters and police came and went from the Borden home at their pleasure.

Revisiting the infamous little ditty:

> *Lizzie Borden took an axe*
> *And gave her mother forty whacks*
> *When she saw what she had done*
> *She gave her father forty-one*

This rhythmically rhetorical rhyme helped to create the myth about Lizzie Borden. Many variables helped to create this myth, such as the media reporting *facts* that were not true but exaggerated just to sell a newspaper. The fact is that each line of this chant is inaccurate. First, the murder weapon was not an axe but most likely a hatchet; this is concluded by a Harvard University scientist who examined the skulls of the victims. It was determined through an analysis of the wound size, shape, and impact that the weapon was smaller than an axe and more consistent to that of a hatchet. On August 4, 1892, the *Boston Daily Globe* ran headlines:

A.J. BORDEN AND WIFE BUTCHERED
BOTH SKULLS CRUSHED AND HEADS HACKED TO PIECES

Within the body of the article it stated:

> The head was covered with wounds from half an inch to six inches in length, and the wall of the skull had been crushed in. One gaping cut extended from the forehead diagonally across the face to the shoulder blade, and had evidently been inflicted by a butchers [sic] cleaver or broadaxe.

On the same day of the murder that occurred between 9:30 a.m. and 11:15 a.m., these news reports already began to report *facts* without the investigation being complete or even barely started.

Second, Abby Borden was not murdered with forty whacks. According to a variety of sources, the actual number of wounds to Abby Borden is between eighteen to twenty-one. Embellishment of the description of wounds to both victims is easy when the press reports its information in such detail. Third, the chant implies immediacy when it states "and when she saw what she had done." It is implied that after the murderer realized what he/she did, immediately Andrew was murdered. In fact, as testimony states, there is an hour and a half between both murders. However, as mentioned earlier, some contemporary scholars are beginning to dispute the time between the deaths of both of the victims. Lastly, as supported through scientific testimony, Andrew Borden was not murdered by forty-one whacks but with between nine and eleven impact wounds.

After a reconsideration of the familiar chant, it is clear that the information is totally false. To get as close to the "truth" as we can, an objective examination of primary sources must be made. This, however, does not mean that the truth will be revealed because too much information may have been initially lost. What it does mean is that we can find some truths with the information we do have if we explore the case in a fashion that accommodates contingencies and requires critical thinking skills designed to effectively gather information, evaluate it, analyze it, and synthesize it, which may lead to new interpretive possibilities and a richer understanding.

Facts and inferences are often comingled in accounts of this case. What we do know is that thousands of people came to stand outside the home as the investigation commenced. John Morse returned from his morning outing and saw hundreds of people outside. He remained outside eating several pears before entering the home to find out what occurred that caused the mass attention to the Borden household.

The fact is that the investigation was flawed and incomplete. The investigation failed to find any direct evidence linking Lizzie to the crime. Yet, Lizzie was charged with the crime of murder for the deaths of Andrew and Abby Borden; in fact, just to be certain, when the indict-ment was handed down, she was charged with three counts of murder, one for Andrew Jackson Borden, one for Abby Durfee Borden, and one charge for both of them—just to make sure the charge stuck.

There were four official proceedings during the aftermath of the murder and investigation: the inquest, a preliminary hearing, a grand jury review, and a criminal trial. Lizzie testified only at the inquest. In fact, at that time, it was customary, according to Massachusetts state law, that witnesses be informed of their right to counsel before any legal proceeding if the person is a suspect in the case. But because Lizzie was not advised that she did have a right to counsel at the inquest, as she was the main [and only] suspect, her inquest testimony was not admissible at her trial. Now let's look at a rhetorical inquiry of this case through the lens of Kenneth Burke's rhetorical theory as it offers a consideration of motive, mystery, propaganda, and the scapegoating embedded within the strange case of Lizzie Borden.

REFERENCES

Brown, A. (1992). *Lizzie Borden*. New York: Dell.

Kent, D. (1992). *The Lizzie Borden sourcebook*. Boston: Branden Publishing Company, Inc.

Masterton, W. (2000). *Lizzie didn't do it*. Boston: Branden Publishing Company, Inc.

Veblen, T. (1988/1960). *The theory of the leisure class: The challenging analysis of social conduct that ironically probes misused wealth and conspicuous consumption*. New York: Mentor Books.

CHAPTER 2

LIZZIE BORDEN: A RHETORICAL INQUIRY

This chapter is interested in looking at motives, specifically motives of the authorities who made this case so infamous. Through the lens of several components of Kenneth's Burke rhetorical theory, we can proceed toward a new understanding of the Borden case, one that might shatter the myth of Lizzie Borden's guilt. These aspects include the notion of scapegoat, mystery, propaganda, and Burke's dramatism. By using Burke as our guide, we can ask questions and gain a potential and novel alternate understanding of this unresolved historical conundrum. In this chapter, the following previously published essay stands on its own to open our rhetorical inquiry. This essay was originally published in the *Lizzie Borden Quarterly*[1] and can serve to open our understanding of the complexities in Kenneth Burke's rhetorical thought.

---

[1] Holba, A. (2003). Shattering the myth. *Lizzie Borden Quarterly. 10*(3), 10–18. The only change made to this essay is the citation style from MLA to APA for consistency with the style of this text.

LIZZIE BORDEN:
SHATTERING THE MYTH

The focus of this inquiry is to examine motives surrounding the aftermath of the Borden murders that occurred in Fall River, Massachusetts, August 4, 1892. My intention is not to seek to solve these murders but rather to provide an objective look at the crime, the investigation, and the official inquest transcript testimony of Lizzie Borden through the lens of Kenneth Burke's theory of form and dimensions of his pentad. While there are many unanswered questions that aid in perpetuating this *myth* of Lizzie Borden, this paper entertains only two questions. First, why do the police and prosecutors pursue criminal charges against Lizzie Borden when there is no real link or direct evidence connecting Lizzie to the act of murder? Second, why do women's groups support her during the accusation and trial phase and then demonstrate their disdain after her acquittal?

Burke's theory of form and the dimensions of his pentad enable a discussion of motives that may help to explain *why* certain actions were taken by contemporaries of Lizzie Borden. Assuming there is no need to reconstruct the story of the Borden murders, I begin with introducing Kenneth Burke's theory, and then I address each particular question through the lens of this theory. I also examine aspects of Burke's pentad through lenses of *mystery*, *scapegoat,* and *propaganda*, which enable the consideration of other kinds of motives. It is hoped that by the end of this analysis that the horizon of significance will have diverged, resulting in opening up a range of possibilities to understand the events in Fall River, 1892.

> *Lizzie Borden took an axe*
> *And gave her mother forty whacks*
> *When she saw what she had done*
> *She gave her father forty-one*

KENNETH BURKE:
DIMENSIONS OF THE PENTAD

To understand *why* people are moved to a particular action, Kenneth Burke stated there are five terms, which are generating principles of motives;

they are act, scene, agent, agency, and purpose (Burke, 1969). This pentad has four parts, which are the indicative (act-scene), the poetic (agent), the rhetorical (agency), and the ethical (purpose, *religious*) (Thames, 2002). In the case of the Borden murders, the indicative is the factual basis which is represented through transcripts of official testimony. The poetic, in this case, would include the ditty, whereby Lizzie Borden's contemporaries are the agents of the lyric. There is some internal consistency as it is based upon an actual event and can be contained within itself, as it has no other purpose other than to rhyme a little ditty about a particular event. On the other hand, according to Thames (2002), Burke says that every linguistic action will contain all the elements of the pentad. Therefore, while this can stand alone as an element of the pentad, it can also function as a linguistic act with a rhetorical purpose, to alleviate the fear surrounding this heinous crime (Thames, 2002).

Another linguistic act within the poetic dimension would include the 1975 movie, *The Legend of Lizzie Borden*, from Paramount Pictures. This is a movie made to purely entertain, so it can stand on its own. However, it can also be viewed as containing all the dimensions of the pentad. After significant factual events were withheld from the movie, could it be the director's intention to dissuade viewers from drawing a particular conclusion about the crimes? These types of questions can be applied to all the other poetic forms of linguistic acts, such as operas, musicals, and dramas.

This poetic appeal leads naturally to the rhetorical dimension of Burke's pentad. This dimension looks at *why* people do things. Why was the movie written the way it was, to exclude extremely important factual basis data? Why was the little ditty written to rhyme like a Mother Goose nursery rhyme? Why were reporters paying people to lie and publish false reports in daily newspapers? How could it be that the police failed to ask general information questions, basic to any inquiry, from partic-ular people connected with Andrew Borden? Why did women's groups support Lizzie Borden's cause during her trial and not afterwards? Many of these questions then lead into the next dimension, the ethical. While some people may have been led to their action through straight rhetorical matters, such as the historical moment, there could also be another reason, an ethical dilemma. This dimension of ethics concerns more what is right from wrong than the poetic dimension, but it is a natural extension of each of the other dimensions.

Burke (1969) doesn't stop with identifying these principles of motives. He continues that they work together and not necessarily in an equal capacity; he calls this the *range of ratios*. He says that, "[r]atios are principles of determination" (1969, p. 15). This means that one dimension of the pentad may be more evident than another, although still implicitly ever present. For example, Burke says that by a scene-act ration he means "that the nature of the act is implicit, or analogously present, in the nature of the scene" (1969, p. 444). So these dimensions work with each other, whether implicitly or explicitly and it is natural for them to, at times, subsume each other.

Burke's pentad basically tells us how an orientation happens. He says it involves interpretation and this is where the dimension of motives begins. In *Permanence and Change*, Burke says that interpretation "affects the nature of communication, of the 'technological psychosis' that has developed out of magic and religion" (1984, p. 3). There are always motives behind each act in which we engage; this motive is our orientation. In critical analysis of a linguistic act, "invention is the mother of necessity: the very power of criticism has enabled man to build up cultural structures so complex that still greater powers of criticism are needed" (Burke, 1984, p. 5). In fact, Burke continues that "we not only interpret the character of events…we may also interpret our interpretations" (Burke, 1984, p. 6).

From this point I consider two questions to determine how they connect to this Burkean pentad. While there are other methods of criticism that may also highlight the *why* and *how*, this paper is limited to the Burke paradigm.

Question One

The first question deals with why the police and prosecutors pursued criminal charges against Lizzie Borden when they knew and subsequently admitted that there was no real link or direct evidence to connect Lizzie with the murder. Burke's theory of form can help to understand this phenomenon. First, he says "form is the creation of an appetite in the mind of the auditor, and the adequate satisfying of that appetite" (1968,

p. 31). He then explains that form involves a "communicative relationship between a writer and an audience, with both parties actively participating" (1973, p. 329). This relationship leads to an expectation as the form "involves a momentary frustration between the promise of an event and the fulfillment of its actualization" (Swartz, 1996, p. 313). When Burke argues that form leads his audience to anticipate another part of the form, this explains why the police tried to remain true the form of the case solvency. In particular, from the beginning of the police involvement at the Borden murder scene, the focus was directed on Lizzie Borden as the suspect because she preferred to refer to Abby as her stepmother rather than her mother. Lizzie made this clarification to police who were questioning her at the time. The officer, however judgmental, believed that this clarification indicated that there was trouble between Lizzie and Abby, which obviously meant that Lizzie killed her. According to the testimony of Marshal Fleet, he asked Lizzie who would want to kill her mother, Lizzie quickly corrected him as to Abby's biological deficiency:

> Do you know of anyone who might have killed your father or mother?

> She is *not* my mother, sir. She is my stepmother. My mother died when I was a child (Kent, 1992a, p. 21).

This theme would resurface throughout the investigation. Actually, it guided the investigation. From this point in the investigation, which was later that same day, the investigation seemed to focus on proving that Lizzie was guilty of the crime. With this narrow vision many bits of information were overlooked because police believed that Lizzie was guilty, therefore, nothing else mattered. According to Burke's notion of form, the patriarchal authority charged with the responsibility to solve the crime needed to pursue Lizzie as the perpetrator simply because Lizzie deviated from their norm as she indicated, in what they perceived as defiance to social norms, that Abby Borden was not her mother.

Now, the historical moment must also be considered because today that statement would be welcomed by any official investigator, as it would have clarified information, rather than be seen as "unfitting" to say. According to Mary Shanley (1989), historian in gender studies, "women presided over the home, while men sallied forth into the public realm" (p. 3). Additionally, she says, "the family was a locus of male power sustained by the judicial authority of the state" (p. 4). As far as the duties in which women were expected to engage, Shanley says, "In addition to bearing children, middle class women directed and working class women performed, the work involved maintaining the household—care of the children, sewing, cooking, and cleaning" (p. 5). Generally, women had a place in society that was socially constructed by the male-dominated culture.

In Lizzie's case, she did not work outside the home. Her father was a respectable businessman and had several thriving business ventures to occupy his time. Lizzie did not need to work for financial reasons but spent her time teaching Sunday school and participating in volunteer activities with the local chapter of a Women's Christian Temperance League. Not much is factually known about her romantic interests. Lizzie was thirty-two years old, unmarried, and living at home with her father, sister, Emma, stepmother, and maid, Bridget Sullivan.

Knowing this history and being one hundred years later, there is no reason to believe the statement to Fleet to be suspicious. However, in August of 1892, that statement, coming from a woman, was simply against the norm. In the eyes of male-dominated society Lizzie had erred against the institution of family and the hierarchy of patriarchal authority. Once this statement was made the criminal investigation settled in upon Lizzie Andrew Borden and the officials remained true to their form of the linguistic action of family, as they knew their murderess and would stop at nothing to prove it.

Another attack to the patriarchal form was the rising women's movement at the time. The Suffragists were gaining attention and this attack on form, as patriarchy might have seen it, led them to struggle to remain intact to their form of social norms. They could not imagine a daughter, now a spinster according to social norms, would openly and publicly deny her father's chosen second wife. It was not a daughter's place to do so, therefore, the police had to conform the situation to their social norms. In this case, she had to be the killer, and they had to make her the killer.

This was subsequently demonstrated after the Knowlton papers (sealed documents from the case) were released by the estate of Hosea Knowlton, prosecutor. In these papers, a letter was revealed from Knowlton to the (then) Attorney General Pillsbury, which said:

> I note your suggestions about form of indictment which I will adopt if we ever get so far: of which, however, I am far from certain (Kent, 1992a, Centerfold).

A second memo indicated:

> Personally I would like very much to get rid of the trial of the case, and fear that my own feelings in that direction may have influenced my better judgment...I confess, however, I cannot see my way clear to any disposition...even though there is reasonable expectation of a verdict (Kent, 1992a, Centerfold).

So once the investigation slanted towards Lizzie, the prosecution *manipulated* evidence, all to conform to their *form*. For example, the hatchet found in the basement was led, by police, to be the murder weapon. The media presented many articles about the hatchet found in the Borden basement and how it was linked to Lizzie and the crime. However, upon scientific investigation by Harvard scientists, it was determined the one hatchet with blood on it was not even human blood. Knowlton just assumed that the scientific testimony would conform to his assumption about the murder weapon, so he did not interview the Harvard witness prior to taking the stand at the trial. It was during the witness's direct testimony to the prosecution that it was revealed not to be human blood. It seems the prosecution made too many assumptions in an attempt to meet the anticipated form, that Lizzie was their murderer.

So far, the examples provided meet with Burke's notion of form as "enabl[ing] us to experience in [a particular] way" (1968, p. 143). This artistic form, applied to this particular case, constructs a situation and Burke's theory "explains that the artists must create certain situational variables within his/her plot, variables suggesting to an audience the plausibility of a particular resolution" (Swartz, 1996, p. 313). In

Burke's pentad, the behavior and expectations of the police/prosecution can be looked upon through the lens of the rhetorical. What did make these men make these particular assumptions? How could they be driven so blindly by this anticipated form? Lloyd Bitzer (1968), in his article, "The Rhetorical Situation," argues that "rhetorical discourse is called into existence by situation [and that…] the situation dictates the significant physical and verbal responses; and…it constrains the words which are uttered" (p. 11). Bitzer continues that the perceptions of the rhetor do not necessarily shape, define, or lend character to the situation but they account for mistakes of the rhetor. He also argues that these are misperceptions by the rhetor. In this case, the police and prosecutor were guided by misperception.

While this analysis could continue for pages, I must limit this inquiry into one more example. An inquest is an official legal proceeding and is an investigative tool utilized by the District Attorney to find evidence of a crime. It was called on Tuesday, August 9, 1892, just five days after the murders. It lasted three days and Lizzie testified each day, along with a select few other witnesses. Upon examination of the inquest testimony, there are numerous issues raised in this matter. The issues include:

1. The District Attorney knowingly questions Lizzie when she is his main suspect. He denies her right to counsel [according to Massachusetts State law in 1892]
2. The DA badgered the witness [Lizzie] as his frustration mounted
3. The DA failed to follow through with appropriate investigatory questions
4. And the myth of Lizzie's *inconsistent* testimony or, as Knowlton described it, her *confession,* was crafted.

This testimony is direct from the inquest testimony given by Lizzie Borden. It is interesting that this is dubbed as Lizzie Borden's *confession*, at the time and today, by people who believe Lizzie guilty. It is also interesting that, to this date, no other inquest testimony from any other witness is known to exist.

When Lizzie was ordered to the inquest, Knowlton had an arrest warrant for her, signed and ready to be executed (Kent, 1992a, p. 46). But there was not enough evidence to support that warrant for a trial; therefore, he needed to try to obtain additional evidence from the inquest. It was Judge Blaisdell's duty to inform Lizzie of her right to counsel, but his excuse was that he thought the prosecutor informed her (Brown, 1991). This mistake should never have occurred. Both Knowlton and Blaisdell had many years of experience and a mistake this large should have not been acceptable. This was a denial of Lizzie's rights afforded to her under Massachusetts State law that had a protection clause similar to Miranda, as we know it (Brown, 1991).

The most documented inquest issue is that of Lizzie's inconsistent testimony or her *confession*, as it has been labeled. Examiners of the inquest transcript suggest Lizzie lied when she answered questions regarding Morse's habit of visiting the Borden residence, about her whereabouts when Andrew came home the morning of the murders, and her whereabouts during the time of the murders. I submit that Lizzie did not lie at this proceeding but was still under the influence of morphine sulfate and somewhat confused about details. Apparently, after the discovery of the murders, Dr. Bowen sedated Lizzie due to the trauma of discovering her father murdered. At the trial, defense counsel cross-examined Dr. Bowen relative to this issue:

Q. Did you have occasion to prescribe for her on account of this mental distress and nervous excitement, after that?
A. Yes sir.
Q. When was it?
A. Friday.
Q. Was the prescription or medicine the same as the other?
A. It was different.
Q. What was it?
A. Sulphate of morphine.
Q. In what doses?
A. One eighth of a grain.
Q. When?

A. Friday night at bedtime.

Q. The next day you changed that?

A. I did not change the medicine but doubled the dose.

Q. That was on Saturday?

A. On Saturday.

Q. Did you continue the dose on Sunday?

A. Yes sir.

Q. Did you continue it on Monday?

A. Yes sir.

Q. And on Tuesday?

A. Yes sir.

Q. How long did she continue to have that?

A. She continued to have that all the time she was in the station house.

Q. After her arrest, was it not?

A. And before.

Q. In other words, she had it all the time up to the time of her arrest, the hearing and while in the station house?

A. Yes sir.

Q. Does not morphine, given in double doses to allay mental distress and nervous excitement, somewhat affect the memory and change and alter the view of things and give people hallucinations?

A. Yes sir. (Kent, 1992a, p. 109)

This confirms the heavy dosage of morphine that Lizzie had been given and indicates she was still under its influence at the inquest proceeding. Therefore, the following areas of *inconsistent* testimony are more likely the result of her being drugged rather than lying.

From the inquest testimony, there were several areas where Lizzie did not provide precise answers. When Knowlton questioned Lizzie regarding coming downstairs the morning of the murders, he asked Lizzie about her conversation with Bridget:

Q. Tell us again what time you came downstairs.

A. It was a little before nine, I should say. About quarter. I don't know sure…

Q. Did you say anything to Maggie?

A. I did not.

Q. Did you say anything about washing the windows?

A. No sir.

Q. Did you speak to her?

A. I think I told her I did not want any breakfast.

Q. You do not remember about talking about washing the windows?

A. I don't remember whether I did or not. I don't remember it. Yes, I remember. Yes, I asked her to shut the parlor blinds when she got through because the sun was so hot. [Inquest Day 1] (Kent, 1992b, p. 64)

Knowing Lizzie had been under so much influence of morphine, her answers seem only appropriate. There should be more concern if her answers had been rehearsed, prepared, and memorized.

Critics of Lizzie suggest that she lied when she testified about her whereabouts when her father left and returned home that morning. But the testimony should speak for itself:

Q. How long was your father gone?

A. I don't know that.

Q. Where were you when he returned?

A. I was down in the kitchen.

Q. What doing?

A. Reading an old magazine that had been left in the cupboard, an old Harper's magazine.

Q. Had you got through ironing?

A. No sir.

Q. Had you stopped ironing?

A. Stopped for the flats.

Q. Were you waiting for them to be hot?

A. Yes sir.

Q. Was there a fire in the stove?

A. Yes sir.

Q. When your father went away, you were ironing then?

A. I had not commenced, but was getting the little ironing board and the flannel.

Q. Are you sure you were in the kitchen when your father returned?

A. I am not sure whether I was there or in the dinning room. (Kent, 1992b, p. 65)

Then the testimony modulates to whether Lizzie was upstairs or downstairs at the time Andrew returned:

Q. Did you spend any time up the front stairs before your father returned?

A. No sir.

Q. Or after he returned?

A. No sir. I did stay in my room long enough when I went up to sew a little piece of tape on a garment.

Q. Was that the time when your father came home?

A. He came home after I came downstairs.

Q. You were not upstairs when he came home?

A. I was not upstairs when he came home, no sir.

Q. What was Maggie doing when your father came home?

A. I don't remember whether she was there or whether she had gone upstairs. I can't remember.

Q. Who let your father in?

A. I think he came to the front door and rang the bell and I think Maggie let him in and he said he had forgotten his key. So I think she must have been downstairs...

Q. Where were you when the bell rang?

A. I think in my room upstairs.

Q. Then you were upstairs when your father came home?

A. I don't know sure, but I think so.

Q. What were you doing?

A. As I say, I took up these clean clothes and stopped and basted a little piece of tape on a garment.

Q. Did you come down before your father was let in?

A. I was on the stairs coming down when she let him in...

Q. You remember Miss Borden, I will call your attention to it so as to see if I have any misunderstanding, not for the purpose of confusing you, you remember that you told me several times that you were downstairs and not upstairs when your father came home? You have forgotten perhaps?

A. I don't know what I have said. I have answered so many questions and I am so confused I don't know one thing from another. I am telling you just as nearly as I know...

A. I think I was downstairs in the kitchen. (Kent, 1992b, p. 66)

Later, Knowlton questioned Lizzie in the same fashion regarding what she had been doing in the barn at the time of the murders.

Q. How long did you remain there?

A. I don't know. Fifteen or twenty minutes.

Q. What doing?

A. Trying to find lead for a sinker.

Q. What made you think there would be lead for a sinker up there?

A. Because there was some there.

Q. Was there not some by the door?

A. Some pieces of lead by the open door but there was a box full of old things upstairs.

Q. Did you bring any sinker back from the barn?

A. Nothing but a piece of chip I picked up on the floor...

Q. Had you got a fish line?

A. Not here. We had some at the farm.

Q. Had you got a fishhook?

A. No sir.

Q. Had you got any apparatus for fishing at all?

A. Yes. Over there.

Q. Had you any sinkers over there?

A. I think there were some. It is so long since I have been there, I think there were some.

Q. You had no reason to suppose you were lacking sinkers?

A. I don't think there were any on my lines. (Kent, 1992b, p. 76)

This questioning continued until Knowlton, in trying to show Lizzie a liar, appeared to be frustrated with his lack of listening skills.

Q. It occurred to you after your father came in it would be a good time to go to the barn after sinkers and you had no reason to suppose there was not an abundance of sinkers at the farm and an abundance of lines?

A. The last time I was there, there were some lines.

Q. Did you not say before you presumed there were sinkers at the farm?

A. I don't think I said so.

Q. You did say so exactly. Do you now say you presume there were not sinkers at the farm?

A. I don't think there were any fishing lines suitable to use at the farm. I don't think there were any sinkers on any line that had been mine.

Q. Do you remember telling me you presumed there were lines and sinkers and hooks at the farm?

A. I said there were lines, I thought perhaps hooks. I did not say I thought there were sinkers on my lines. There was another box of lines over there beside mine.

Q. You thought there were not sinkers?

A. Not on my lines. (Kent, 1992b, p. 76)

This demonstrates that while Lizzie may seem confused, she is not inconsistent. Lizzie had not changed her story but clarified it. Knowlton would hear her answers as he wanted to hear them and appeared to only hear what he believed he could use to confuse the witness. This only adds to his frustrations. A few questions later, Knowlton's frustration projected:

Q. What was the use of telling me a while ago you had no sinkers on your line at the farm?

A. I thought I made you understand that those lines at the farm were no good to use.

Q. Did you not mean for me to understand one of the reasons you were searching for sinkers was that the lines you had at the farm, as you remembered then, had no sinkers on them?

A. I said the lines at the farm had no sinkers.

Q. I did not ask you what you said. Did you not mean for me to understand that?

A. I meant for you to understand I wanted the sinkers and was going to have new lines. (Kent, 1992b, p. 77)

Another area of questioning where it is apparent that Knowlton did not carefully listen to Lizzie's answer is when he questioned her about what she did upstairs prior to Andrew returning home that morning. The second day of questioning, Knowlton inquired as to what Lizzie did that morning in question:

Q. You mean you went up there to sew a button on?

A. I basted a piece of tape on.

Q. Do you remember you did not say that yesterday?

A. I don't think you asked me. I told you yesterday I went upstairs directly after I came up from down cellar, with the clean clothes. (Kent, 1992b, p. 72)

Lizzie is correct. On the first day of the testimony, Lizzie answered

A. No sir. I did stay in my room long enough when I went up to sew a little piece of tape on a garment. (Kent, 1992b, p. 65)

It is clear that Lizzie remembered this correctly. It seems that Knowlton wanted to hear something other than to what Lizzie testified. He is doing everything he can to confuse the issue and portray Lizzie as a liar. He is trying to match the anticipated form that would lead to a particular anticipated end result.

There were times in Knowlton's questioning that he did not follow through with the next appropriate question. This leads one to believe that either Knowlton did not want to pursue the issue or he did not see the issue. In asking Lizzie if she was aware of anyone who was on bad terms with her father, Knowlton did not pursue the answer he was given.

> Q. Besides that, do you know of anybody that your father had bad feelings toward or who had bad feelings toward your father?
> A. I know of one man who has not been friendly with him. They have not been friendly for years.
> Q. Who?
> A. Mr. Hiram C. Harrington.
> Q. What relation is he to him?
> A. He is my father's brother-in-law.
> Q. Your mother's brother?
> A. My father's only sister married Mr. Harrington.
> Q. Anybody else that was on bad terms with your father or that your father was on bad terms with?
> A. Not that I know of. (Kent, 1992b, p. 55)

Knowlton never followed through with an inquiry into why they were on bad terms, which would have been a normal course of questioning.

Knowlton badgered Lizzie throughout her testimony. As he tried to confuse issues and call her a liar, he badgered her to the point where it was obvious that Knowlton thought that this was his last resort effort to solve the murders. He almost appeared to be grasping at straws:

> Q. Can you give me any explanation why all you have told me would occupy more than three minutes?
> A. Yes. It would take me more than three minutes.
> Q. To look in that box you have described the size of on the bench and put down the curtain and then get out as soon as you conveniently could; would you say you were occupied in that business 20 minutes?
> A. I think so because I did not look at the box when I first went up.

Q. What did you do?

A. I ate my pears.

Q. Stood there eating the pears, doing nothing?

A. I was looking out of the window.

Q. Stood there looking out of the window, eating pears?

A. I should think so.

Q. How many did you eat?

A. Three I think.

Q. You were feeling better than you did in the morning?

A. Better than I did the night before.

Q. You were feeling better than you were in the morning?

A. I felt better in the morning than I did the night before.

Q. That is not what I asked you. You were then, when you were in that hay loft, looking out the window and eating three pears, feeling better, were you not, than you were in the morning when you could not eat any breakfast?

A. I never eat breakfast.

Q. You did not answer my question and you will, if I have to put it all day. Were you then when you were eating those three pears in that hot loft, looking out that closed window, feeling better than you were in the morning when you ate no breakfast?

A. I was feeling well enough to eat the pears.

Q. Were you feeling better than you were in the morning?

A. I don't know how to answer you because I told you I felt better in the morning anyway.

Q. Do you understand my question? My question is whether, when you were in the loft of the barn, you were feeling better than you were in the morning when you got up?

A. No, I felt about the same.

Q. Were you feeling better than you were when you told your mother you did not care for any dinner?

A. No sir. I felt about the same.

Q. Well enough to eat pears, but not well enough to eat anything for dinner?

A. She asked me if I wanted any meat.

Q. I ask you why you should select that place, which was the only
place, which would put you out of sight of the house, to eat
those three pears in? (Kent, 1992b, p. 81)

And so the questioning continued. Knowlton got nowhere but out of
breath in his pursuit of how Lizzie felt and why she could eat the pears
but not dinner. The point he had tried to make just wasn't there but Lizzie
did not lose any ground in that round. It appears the prosecutor dismantled
his own case as it unfolded.

In questioning Lizzie about hypothetical blood found on one of her
skirts, Knowlton tried to confuse Lizzie or say something that he could
use to twist her words, but Lizzie remained intact from this assault.

Q. Did you give the officer the same skirt you had on the day of
the tragedy?
A. Yes sir.
Q. Do you know whether there was any blood on the skirt?
A. No sir.
Q. Assume that there was, do you know how it got there?
A. No sir.
Q. Have you any explanation of how it might come there?
A. No sir.
Q. Did you know there was any blood on that skirt you gave
them?
A. No sir.
Q. Assume that there was. Can you give any explanation of how
it came there on the dress skirt?
A. No sir. (Kent, 1992b, p. 92)

Knowlton continued this useless line of questioning only to waste time
and energy and to attempt to create a red herring. People listening to the
parade of questions might have failed to see the illogic and be drafted on
to Knowlton's bandwagon, thus, participate in the assault on Lizzie.

In the end, after three days of testimony, Judge Blaisdell found that
there was enough evidence to serve the warrant for her arrest, except they
decided to prepare a new one based on her *confession* and *conflicting*

statements. This was only the beginning of the parade of events that would remain in the media attention for the next nine months.

QUESTION TWO

The second question, although related to the first, pertains to why women's groups rallied to Lizzie's side, supporting her through newspaper articles and public rhetoric, but exiled her from their groups after her acquittal. Burke's theory of form can also explain *why* these groups and individual women had these hypocritical reactions.

First, women supported Lizzie through their physical appearances at her trial. "Nearly half of the spectators in the New Bedford court house...are women" reported the *New Bedford Evening Standard*, June 6, 1893 (p. 5). On June 7, 1893, *The New Bedford Mercury* reported:

> The New Bedford man who comes home and finds it deserted, with every outward appearance of a hasty departure on the part of his wife, needn't be alarmed. There has been no elopement; the dear creature is probably in the crowd of morbid females who are storming the door of the county courthouse, trying to get admission to the Borden trial. (p. 4)

The *Fall River Daily Globe* reported, June 9, 1893:

> The real jury of her peers which is trying Lizzie Borden, is the job lot of femininity which fills the jury box on the south side of the New Bedford court house every day. (p. 4)

Private interviews from women active in the women's movement included this statement made to the *New Bedford Daily Mercury*, July 3, 1893:

> This Borden trial, from beginning to end, has been one of the most surprising revelations of the possibilities of gross injustice...is she guilty? No, a thousand times no. There has not been a shred of evidence of guilt. (Rebello, 1999, p. 259)

Mary Livermore reported in the *Fall River Daily Herald*, July 6, 1893:

> *The Fall River Herald* is even yet persisting in scurri-
> lous persecution of her [Lizzie Borden], even though she
> is adjudged innocent by the highest court, persistent in
> going over all the details that District Attorney Knowlton
> went over, with innuendoes, but then it is useless to talk
> of this; it is the sort of journalism, which is entirely
> discreditable (p. 8).

The *New Bedford Evening Journal* reported on July 7, 1893, that "The memory of Lizzie Borden is to be preserved in New Bedford" (p. 8). The article described the newly organized group calling themselves *The Lizzie Borden Entertainment Club*. This was a group that was organized similar to fan clubs of the mid-twentieth century. Their beginning membership started with fifty members. "The object of the club in the words of the constitution is 'to promote the cause of temperance, but at the same time to oppose the so-called prohibition movement of today'" (p. 8). Instead of a gavel for their meetings, a hatchet was used in its place. Many other Lizzie clubs were formed, such as *Lizzie Borden's Friends' Organize* and *The Society of the Friends of Lizzie Borden*. Today, the *Lizzie Borden International Association*, formed in April 1995, continues the preserva-tion and supports advanced studies into the Borden mystery.

However, after the acquittal and after the initial supportive reaction, these opinions began to change. The *Fall River Daily Globe* reported, June 4, 1894, that:

> Lizzie did not like the treatment she received by some of
> its members [Woman's Christian Temperance League].
> "Many times she met her old associates in the street and
> they quietly pass[ed] her with out a sign of recognition…
> Since her release, it is alleged that many of the members
> have cut her dead". Lizzie never attended any of the
> meetings after she was acquitted. "It has been known that
> individual members spoke as if they would ostracize her
> socially if she did" (Rebello, 1999, p. 293).

Newspapers continued to air the private interactions between Lizzie Borden and her contemporaries. She even had school children taunting her on her own property for which she complained to the police (Rebello, 1999, p. 299). But in the end, Lizzie returned society's coldness. She moved to a larger home but stayed within the city of Fall River. She no longer attended her former social outlets but created new ones and new friends (p. 310).

It seems clear that the support for Lizzie during her ordeal was omnipotent but afterward it was nowhere to be found from her female peers. Burke may provide insight into why women reacted in this manner. First, the event was over. During the trial while the women rallied to Lizzie's support, the men were believed this support wasn't due to their earnest adoration for Lizzie, but it was due to them being "morbidly curious…wasting time in the court room" (Rebello, 1999, p. 225). One man reported in the *New Bedford Evening Standard*, June 20, 1893, that "all women hereabouts seem to have made up their minds that Lizzie Borden is guilty. They don't think that she cried enough" (p. 4). So men in society had to justify this peculiar attraction the women had for the case, but they could not believe that their women actually supported Lizzie. In fact, they seemed to trivialize the response that the women had to this case. On the other hand, women's voices were not really being heard as clearly as they should have. Thereby, when it came to getting back to a "normal" society, women again conformed to the male hierarchy mindset. So, women's groups did not conform to the anticipated response that male social standards suggested. But the male response was blinded by their anticipated form as well. Therefore, there was no other response that women's groups could have reverted back to after the attraction of this infamous trial.

Another perspective to consider why women reacted with such disdain after the trial ended in acquittal is driven by the women's movement in that historical moment. Since women's groups rallied for Lizzie and supported her while she was in jail but once acquitted they withdrew all such support, this may indicate that more was at stake then just Lizzie's virtue. It almost seems as if Lizzie was good enough to discuss on their political forum, providing publicity, as well as Lizzie being an innocent victim of a patriarchal society, but their support did not extend after her acquittal. Women's groups used Lizzie as propaganda to stir the pot and be a token for their cause. Lizzie and her experiences represented everything that was wrong between men and women. But afterward, women had no platform to stand upon. The case was over. They won and Lizzie was free. Now, Lizzie could only hurt their cause, as she was considered the woman who got away with murder. Too much attention from Lizzie Andrew Borden might now ruin the women's cause, as she was a murderess, a woman who stepped too far outside her social role. When the dust settled, men were still in charge, hierarchy was intact, and the women's cause returned to being mere rhetoric.

BURKE AND MYSTERY

Burke recognized the need for mystery in communication. According to John Meyer (1996), in his article, "Seeking Organizational Unity: Building Bridges in Response to Mystery," he argues there are three sources of mystery; separation, strangeness, and hierarchy. He says that that Burke recognized this need for mystery in communication as it is manifested in ambiguity and contradiction. Meyer argues that mystery is "necessary" to maintain form and maintenance in organizations. He also argues that mystery is essential to enhance communication. Therefore, "in seeking to make the strange familiar, people communicate both in response to it and about it" (p. 210). This is what the women's groups did in order to make sense out of the Borden phenomenon. Meyer continues that while mystery "provokes communication between persons, it also distorts or prevents understanding" (p. 211). Additionally, Meyer says, "people constantly strive to overcome mystery and create order by communicating to form social organization" (p. 211). When it benefited the women's groups to support they did, and this was their attempt to overcome the mystery and keep their unity intact. However, once acquitted, they may have felt as though Lizzie would ultimately hurt their cause as the mystery swayed towards this myth propagated by the *ditty* that assumes Lizzie's guilt. In this way, women needed to return to their form prior to August 4, 1892. According to Meyer, "one can try to overcome separateness by trying to identify with another person or with a group" (p. 213). This may have been their only saving grace in their eyes. Meyer also suggests that this social drama contains power relations and symbolic action and interaction, which is played out manifesting the social structure. This reveals hierarchy and in hierarchy grows a "trained incapacity" (p. 215). Burke (1984) used Veblen's concept of "trained incapacity" as "the state of affairs whereby one's very abilities can function as blindness" (p. 7). This *trained incapacity* seems evident with the police and prosecution, as well as women supporters of Lizzie. It seems they all needed to find a way to understand this mystery at various different times subsequent to the crime. The only way to understand would be to remain within one's power group and succumb to the hierarchy in place. For this reason, people interpreted through their socially constructed social dramas, regardless of the strangeness or ambiguity present within the circumstances. This led people to react particular ways to particular circumstances.

THE SCAPEGOAT

This *trained incapacity*, according to Burke (1984), leads to "the scapegoat mechanism" (p. 17). The issue of Lizzie as a scapegoat fits into both questions. First, according to Burke, a scapegoat is an "error in interpretation" (p. 14). He says, "the scapegoat mechanism in its purest form, [is] the use of a sacrificial receptacle for the ritual unburdening of one's sins…a different orientation to cause and effect" (p.16). This scapegoat is an attempt to reason, but this involves consideration of motives. With respect to the police and prosecution, they expected and judged proper conduct. Their expectancy led to their choice to charge, indict, and try Lizzie. This set of symbol systems that Lizzie encountered were "set up for catharsis by scapegoat" (Burke, 1968, p. 18). This catharsis was the motive for contemporaries involved. But motives change or at least are not fixed (Burke, 1984, p. 25). Specifically regarding the women's groups who showed disdain after their support, Burke would argue, "schemes of motivation change…A motive is not some fixed thing…it is a term of interpretation and being such it will naturally take its place within the framework of our *weltanschauung* as a whole" (1984, p. 25). Burke might also explain their behavior as "the process of rationalization…centered in the entire scheme of judgments as to what people ought to do" (p. 25). For all of Lizzie's contemporaries, "linguistic products are composed of concepts…which select certain relationships as meaningful…these relationships are not realities, they are interpretations of reality—hence different frameworks of interpretation will lead to different conclusions as to what is reality" (Burke, p. 35). In other words, Lizzie's contemporaries were all working within different realities from a multiplicity of frameworks. They were bombarded with separateness, strangeness or ambiguity in linguistic actions, and in a hierarchy of a power structure. Social reality must have been socially constructed on an individual basis, based on anything but the facts or the truth.

THE *DITTY* AS PROPAGANDA

This is not an attempt to find fault or pleasure with the actions and reactions of Lizzie Borden contemporaries, but it is worth attempting to discover *why* people did what they did. Not that any of this should justify a particular action but to understand the historical moment as it was might help to debunk the myth surrounding Lizzie Borden. The myth was generated by a four-lined verse of propaganda that was spewing from the mouths of babes and adults during Lizzie's ordeal. The *ditty:*

> *Lizzie Borden took an axe*
> *And gave her mother forty whacks*
> *When she saw what she had done*
> *She gave her father forty-one*

Ceremonial rhetoric is propaganda. At least its intent is the same as propaganda (Thames, 2002). The above *ditty* is propaganda as it intended to maintain the socially constructed formal structure inherent in the case of Lizzie Borden. This propaganda element falls beneath Burke's pentad in all the dimensions. It is indicative because it is the facts that it contains. It is poetic because on a mass scale, people could remember this enchanted rhyme and it sounded "cute," like a Mother Goose rhyme. This poetic dimension bled into the rhetorical realm, as it was the advertising of the plot. People would sing it, people would remember it, people would believe and continue to believe of Lizzie Borden's guilt. Regardless of the nonfactual basis (see below) it exemplified, people would not care. They could unite behind this rhyme and *understand (interpret)* the mystery, bring resolve to their fears.

The *ditty* is totally false. Line one: It was never proven that Lizzie committed the murders and no murder weapon was ever identified. Merely, the wounds are consistent with blunt force from a hatchet, which is not an axe. Line two: Abby Borden suffered approximately eleven wounds, not *forty whacks*. Line three: There is no immediacy involved in the crime. An hour and a half passed between murders. This line implies an immediacy, which did not exist. Line four: Andrew Borden received between eighteen to twenty-one wounds, not forty-one. So, the complete ditty is a socially constructed piece of propaganda design to amplify people's outrage at this most heinous crime. It is not a true value but served a rhetorical purpose, to persuade people that Lizzie was guilty of the murder of her father and stepmother.

CONCLUSION

So instead of trying to solve the Borden mystery maybe we should continue to examine *why* people acted and reacted as they did. We can learn far more about communication if we stop trying to impose our anticipated form or structure upon the linguistic actions in which we live. Burke was right when he said, "Where ever there is persuasion there is rhetoric. And where ever there is meaning there is persuasion" (Burke, 1955, p. 172).

REFERENCES

Bitzer, L.F. (1968). The rhetorical situation. *Philosophy and Rhetoric.* 1, 1–14.

Brown, A. (1991). *Lizzie Borden: The legend, the truth, the final chapter.* Nashville, TN: Rutledge Hill Press.

Burke, K. (1984). *Permanence and change: An anatomy of purpose.* Berkeley: University of California Press.

Burke, K. (1973). *The philosophy of literary form.* Berkeley: University of California Press.

Burke, K. (1969). *A grammar of motives.* Berkeley: University of California Press.

Burke, K. (1968a). *Counter-statement.* Berkeley: University of California Press.

Burke, K. (1968b). *Language as symbolic action: Essays on life, literature, and method.* Berkeley: University of California Press.

Burke, K. (1964). *Perspectives by incongruity.* Bloomington: Indiana University Press.

Burke, K. (1955). *A rhetoric of motives.* New York: Braziller, Inc.

De Mille, A. (1968). *Lizzie Borden: A dance of death.* Boston: Little Brown and Company.

Engstrom, E. (1991). *Lizzie Borden.* New York: Doherty Associates.

Flynn, R. (1985). Foreword. In Edwin Porter, *The Fall River tragedy: A history of the Borden murders.* Portland, ME: King Philip Publishing Co.

Gustafson, A. (1985). *Guilty or innocent?* New York: Holt, Rinehart and Winston.

History's mysteries: The strange case of Lizzie Borden. (1996). A & E Television Networks. New York: New Video Group.

Hunter, E. (1984). *Lizzie.* New York: Arbor House.

Kent, D. (1992a). *Forty whacks: New evidence in the life and legend of Lizzie Borden.* Emmaus, PA: Yankee Books.

Kent, D. (1992b). *The Lizzie Borden sourcebook.* Boston: Branden Publishing Company, Inc.

Kronenwetter, M. (1986). *Free press v. fair trial*. New York: Franklin Watts.

Lincoln, V. (1967). *A private disgrace: Lizzie Borden by daylight*. New York: G.P. Putnam's and Sons.

Lustgarten, E. (1950). *Verdict in dispute*. New York: Charles Scribner and Sons.

Meyer, J. (1996). Seeking organizational unity: Building bridges in response to mystery. *The Southern Communication Journal. 61*(3), 210–220.

Radin, E. (1961). *Lizzie Borden: The untold story*. New York: Simon & Schuster.

Rappaport, D. (1992). *Be the judge, be the jury: The Lizzie Borden trial*. New York: Harper Collins.

Rebello, L. (1999). *Lizzie Borden past & present: A comprehensive reference to the life and times of Lizzie Borden*. Fall River, MA: Al-Zach Press.

Salibrici, M. (1999). Dissonance and rhetorical inquiry: A Burkean model for critical reading and writing. *Journal of Adolescent and Adult Literacy. 42*(8), 628–637.

Satterthwait, W. (1989). *Miss Lizzie*. New York: St. Martin's Press.

Shanley, M. L. (1989). *Feminism, marriage, and the law in Victorian New England*. Princeton, NJ: Princeton University Press.

Showalter, E. (1997). *Hystories*. New York: Columbia University Press.

Spiering, F. (1984). *Lizzie*. New York: Random House.

Sullivan, R. (1974). *Goodbye Lizzie Borden*. Brattleboro, VT: Stephen Greene Press.

Swartz, O. (1996). Kenneth Burke's theory of form: Rhetoric, art, and cultural analysis. *The Southern Communication Journal. 61*(4), 312–322.

Thames, R. (2002). Seminar on Kenneth Burke: Classroom Lecture, Duquesne University.

Public Information Acknowledgments

The Fall River Herald
The Fall River Daily Globe
The New Bedford Evening Standard
The New Bedford Mercury
The New Bedford Journal

Questions for Discussion
on Chapter 2

These questions include content specific questions and open-ended questions designed to open dialogue connecting Kenneth Burke's rhetorical theory and the case of Lizzie Borden. They are designed as a starting place that permits other questions and discussion to unfold.

1. Identify and describe the five dimensions of Kenneth Burke's pentad.
2. Define scapegoat as Kenneth Burke defines it.
3. Describe Lizzie Borden's "confession." Would this be considered a "confession" today?
4. Describe the impact of this case to the women's movement at the time the crimes occurred.
5. Can you think of other contemporary cases where the issue of "scapegoat" has emerged in mediated representations of a crime?
6. What other recent public/political situations involve issues of mystery and the unknown? How did "mystery" function as a rhetorical trope in that circumstance?
7. Take a current unsolved public crime case and apply Burke's pentad to analyze what you really do know and compare it to what is assumed by the general public. How different or similar are these scenarios? Is there a relationship between the ratios of the pentadic analysis and the outcome of your interpretation of events? If so, what is it?

CHAPTER 3

LIZZIE BORDEN, MEDIA, AND HISTORICITY

This chapter includes an essay previously published in *The Hatchet: Journal of Lizzie Borden Studies* entitled, "Edwin Porter's *The Fall River Tragedy*: A Hermeneutic Entrance into the Borden Mystery" that considers the significance of the historical moment when interpreting mediated artifacts. Before rhetorically examining Edwin Porter's *The Fall River tragedy*, I consider newspaper reports printed during the time of the Borden murders and the aftermath to situate a historical understanding. The First Amendment to the United States Constitution provides for freedom of the press. The reasoning behind this is directly related from the experience of our forefathers while under British rule. When the United States was created the founders wanted to create a new *kind* of country. Therefore, above all, it was important that the press would have freedom regardless of topic and presentation. While freedom of the press is paramount, the printed word is not always truth or based upon truths, which consequently poses a moral obligation to print the truth.

The print resources referred to in this section range from local newspapers in the Boston area down to New York and Philadelphia.[1] There will be representations of pro Lizzie journalism and yellow journalism that uses speculation and sensationalism to try and convict Lizzie in print media. Throughout the representations of this event, police and

---

[1] All newspaper references can be found in Kent, D. (1992). *The Lizzie Borden sourcebook*. Boston: Branden Publishing Company, Inc.

civilians are quoted in print and their word is taken as gospel by the then-inquisitive public. Lizzie, however, does not initially provide interviews to reporters and when she is quoted by do-gooders trying to get into the media frenzy, the reported stories are often later found to be false information. Media attraction to Lizzie Borden followed her throughout her life and beyond her death. The story of Lizzie Borden has become a legend, yet she is invariably misunderstood, as she remains virtually unknown to us even after all these years and all of these newspaper reports.

THE MURDER DISCOVERY

One August 4, 1892, *The Fall River Herald* reported:

SHOCKING CRIME
HACKED TO PIECES AT THEIR HOME
Mr. and Mrs. Borden Lose Their Lives
At The Hands of a Drunken Farm Hand

The body of the article, which was printed the same day as the murders, reported erroneous information starting with the address of the crime scene. The Bordens resided at 92 Second Street, Fall River, Massachusetts but T*he Fall River Herald* reported this to be at 62 Second Street. Assuming that the newspaper reporters knew the Bordens, the wealthiest family in Fall River, this merely could have been a typo. It also indicates that a reporter from *The Fall River Herald* was on the scene before the police and medical personnel:

> A Herald reporter entered the house and a terrible sight met his view. On the lounge in the cozy sitting room on the first floor of the building lay Andrew J. Borden, dead. His face presented a sickening sight. Over the left temple a wound six by four had been made as if the head had been pounded with the dull edge of an axe. The left eye had been dug out and a cut extended the length of the nose.

The article continued to describe finding Abby Borden with the same detailed description of her body. Then the article offers the motive of a Portuguese farmhand who apparently, according to the article, had words with Andrew Borden the day of his murder. This information has no grounding or corroboration. It reports incorrectly that Abby Borden must have caught the killer and was chased upstairs where she met her fate. This places her death after Andrew's death.

> Mrs. Borden was in the room at the time, but was so overcome by the assault that she had no strength to make an outcry. In her bewilderment, she rushed upstairs and went into her room. She must have been followed up by the murderer, and as she was retreating into the furthest corner of the room, she was felled by the deadly axe.

This reporting sounds more like a work of fiction rather than the first reporting about the commission of a crime. The rest of the article reports similar spectacular circumstances of Lizzie's discovery of the bodies and other issues facing this event. The timeline of the crime is incorrectly reported and throughout the article there is information that is suggestive and inflammatory regarding witnesses in the area and possible suspects. Another newspaper that reported the event that same day was *The New York Herald*. Suspicion of Lizzie as the culprit is suggested in the headlines:

HUSBAND AND WIFE MURDERED IN DAYLIGHT
Discovered By Their Daughter
SUSPECTING THE DAUGHTER LIZZIE

While the body of the article suggests that John Morse and Bridget Sullivan are also the initial suspects, the headlines indicate otherwise. The *Boston Daily Globe* placed suspicion on Lizzie on the day following the murders also:

DISCOVERY
A WOMAN INQUIRED FOR POISON
SAID THAT DRUG CLERK IDENTIFIED HER
STRANGE STORY TOLD BY
LIZZIE BORDEN

This story is a catalyst for the increase of theories that would emerge and imply the guilt of Lizzie Borden. The article suggests among other things that Lizzie had problems with her stepmother. It also suggests that Lizzie attempted to purchase poison shortly before the murders. The article also quoted the police as saying that the druggist who reported this could positively identify Lizzie as the woman who tried to purchase poison. However, the testimony of the druggist was later not allowed in the trial because he was not able to identify Lizzie Borden as that particular woman beyond a reasonable doubt and the act of poisoning was an act far removed from the act of murder by axe.

Common in most of the newspaper reports were sketches of the crime scene. These sketches had intricate details such as paintings on the wall, etc. It was clear that the observers would have to be inside the crime scene for quite some time to capture details like these. But consider this, these sketches appeared from the day after the murders. The police maintained that they searched the house on five different occasions, not all in the first 24 hours of the crime. Therefore, the implication follows that the scene was never secured from noninvestigative personnel, leaving the risk of crime scene contamination very high. In fact, it could be argued that if the murder weapon was inside the residence, reporters could have removed it. Another argument could be that a knowing or unknowing civilian right under the nose of police removed evidence linking the murderer to the crime. Failure to secure the crime scene depicts the police investigation as severely flawed.

As time passed, the news reports began to clear up misrepresented facts. On August 7, 1892, three days after the murders, *The New York Herald* reported that Abby had been murdered before Andrew. Headlines captured the attention:

MRS. BORDEN WAS DEAD
A FULL HOUR BEFORE
HER HUSBAND CAME.
Developments at Fall River Show
That Mr. Borden Returned Home
To Be Murdered Long After
His Wife Had Been Killed.
The Murderer Must Have Remained in
The House Waiting for His Second
Victim and in Constant
Danger of Discovery.

This would be fascinating news to people following every bit of information they could find. The body of the article depicted police as being bewildered and at a loss for direction.

> Policemen, owl-like and solemn, made a cordon all day around the queer old house where on Thursday a harmless old man and his wife were so cruelly butchered. All day other policemen, equally owl-like and equally silent, careered over the town on a kind of hopeless hunting…Yet at the end of their day of inscrutable labors they knew apparently no more about the murder of A.J. Borden and his wife than they knew at the beginning, and no more than the crowds that gaped all day over the palings about the gruesome house.

Whether this means that a police rope was secured around the residence or more likely that baffled police were aimlessly walking the property three days after the murders in search of some type of clue or evidence, it is clear that the perception presented by news reports suggested that the police investigative personnel were in need of direction. A lot of information had already passed through the printing presses and much of it had been unsubstantiated. There was a report of dissention among the police officials involved in this investigation. *The Fall River Herald* felt the need to set the tables straight:

A great deal of nonsense has been printed about the
Borden murder mystery, but hardly anything equals the
foolish statements that the muddle between the mayor and
the combination over the police appointments has inter-
fered with the investigation. No basis has been afforded
for the report. The police are obeying orders from the
marshal, and every member of the department who has
been assigned a task has discharged it faithfully. There is
no shirking, nobody is grumbling. If dissatisfaction was
apparent to correspondents, it is not extraordinary that
nobody else has perceived it?

This is a response to an article in *The New York Herald* that suggested
the police were bickering among themselves, and it identifies a power
struggle to control the investigation among the Mayor, Chief of Police
and other political representatives. Now, not only are the police losing
focus on the task at hand, but also the media have too.

In the middle of all the official disruption, *The Boston Herald*
printed an article on August 6, 1892 that represented the life of Lizzie
Borden. This is the feminist perspective on Lizzie. In all fairness, the
article suggests that in all the reporting of the murder and the suspicion
surrounding Lizzie, she is presented to the public through the male eyes.
This article shows Lizzie in her personal sphere, her domestic sphere
that allows for a little of the myth of Lizzie Borden to be moved into a
more self-relating light. What we find out about Lizzie is that she was
a strong woman with a lot of personal charm. As a student Lizzie was
described as brilliant. A musician, a philanthropist, a Christian woman
with impeccable morals, the article argues that there was not one unkind
act ever committed by Lizzie.

Other articles of support surfaced on occasion. It should be noted
that most of the articles in support of Lizzie were a few sentences long
but the incriminating articles often took up two and three columns if not
pages of the papers. Some samples of supporting articles are:

The Newport Observer:
Certainly, their star chambered procedure is a little
calculated to inspire public confidence in their course

in treating Miss Borden as an accused and at the same time denying her the advice of counsel and friends in order to scrape together enough circumstantial evidence to warrant the arrest. The interest of a community and of every member in it requires that in all judicial proceedings, especially in those of a criminal nature, there should be the fullest publicity.

The New Bedford Journal:

It must be presumed that the inquest in The Borden case has brought out some important facts not yet in the possession of the public, otherwise it is hardly conceivable that the authorities could have decided to arrest Miss Borden. The arrest deepens rather than lessens the mystery. The young woman may know more about the murders than she tells, but that she should herself have struck the fatal blow seems to us impossible.

The Providence Journal:

If the Fall River police want to find the real criminal in the Borden case they had better keep a sharp eye on the newspaper correspondents who are there. A Boston contemporary publishes pictures of them and we are free to say that we have seldom seen a more villainous looking lot. The only consoling reflection is that perhaps these alleged portraits do not do the subjects full justice.

The Providence Journal (regarding the court proceedings):

It will be time enough to blame the authorities at Fall River when it is shown that they have made a serious blunder. The Borden case is a difficult one, despite the jaunty way in which the newspaper counsel for the defense talk about it, and whether Miss Borden be innocent or not, it was inevitable that she should fall under suspicion-a result for which a curious combination of circumstances was alone responsible. Nothing will be lost, at any rate, by waiting for her acquittal by due process of law.

The Lowell Times:
In our judgment, if the Fall River authorities have erred, the error has been not in being slothful or inactive, but in sticking too closely to the first impression that a member of the household must be the guilty one. That Lizzie Borden is guilty can only be accepted after every other possibility is exploded [sic], and even then it must rest on something much more tangible than anything now known.

The Lowell Times (regarding the State's evidence):
The government case fails at too many points to establish guilt beyond a reasonable doubt or even beyond insuperable doubt…On the whole, the indications are that the accused may be held for the grand jury. But it remains that she can never be convicted by a jury on any evidence which has yet appeared.

After testimony from the preliminary hearing, on August 30, 1892, *The Boston Advertiser* headlines read:

THE TIDE TURNS
LIZZIE BORDEN'S HOPES
MUCH BRIGHTER

The article is lengthy and suggests that the evidence submitted to and testified about cannot adequately link her to the crime. It seems that the further the state (prosecution) went in its presentation of their case, the worse it looked for them as they appeared to be dismantling their own prosecution, successfully.

Once it was apparent that Lizzie had been arrested, news reports continued their obsessive interest. The arrest of Lizzie Borden occurred after the three-day inquest. *The Fall River Herald* explained the events leading up to the arrest:

This inquiry lasted three days and was minute and exhaustive. Judge Blaisdell heard the evidence and so did District Attorney Knowlton, two keen legal minds, and when they looked into the case they said that the theory already adopted by the police was so apparently correct that they were justified in holding the person whom they suspected to be guilty of the atrocious crime. Quickly the decision was reached and no time was lost in carrying out the determination.

This suggests that the District Attorney and the Judge had exhausted all evidence and then acted swiftly to arrest to guilty party. Unfortunately, District Attorney Knowlton had discussions with the Attorney General of Massachusetts unbeknown to the public at the time regarding the truth about his case against Lizzie, and he admitted that it is a case being tried in the press and they needed to move quickly, on behalf of the influence of print media, not actual evidence. In this letter contained in a collection called the Knowlton Papers, Knowlton admitted to knowing the state's case was insufficient to connect Lizzie Borden to the murders. In response to a letter from the defense counsel declining Lizzie be subjected to an insanity examination, Knowlton wrote to Attorney General Pillsbury:

> I did not have time to write so fully as I desired about the insanity business. I could do nothing whatever with Jennings. He took exactly the position I feared he would, and seemed to regard it as some sort of a surrender if he consented to anything. We can make some investigations into the family matters without him, but it will not be so thorough as it would be if we had his assistance. I note your suggestions about form of indictment, which I will adopt if we ever get so far; of which, however, I am far from certain.

Knowlton admitted here, in his letter dated November 22, 1892, that his hands are tied and that he realized the case against Lizzie might not hold up on merits of its own. He also sounded frustrated with the defense strategy because it did not agree with his suggested course of action.

CARVING OUT PUBLIC OPINION

To present some of the ways that the news reports influenced public opinion, the following are excerpts from area newspapers that reported the news of the preliminary hearing, evidence issues, and trial events. On August 12, 1892, in *The New York Times,* headlines read:

Lizzie Borden in Jail

SHE PLEADED NOT GUILTY OF
MURDER WHEN ARRAIGNED
IN COURT

The body of the article remained fairly objective as to the event of the arrest of Lizzie. But it also reported inaccurately that the police had the murder weapon in their possession:

> It is said to-night that the police have in their possession the hatchet which it is supposed was used in killing the Bordens.

While the police were not aware at the time that the hatchet they had was not the murder weapon, reporting this bit could have been more accurate if the term "alleged" or "unconfirmed" was utilized.

The New York Herald reported on August 12, 1892 that Lizzie was formally charged with this crime. But the *Herald* reported Jennings scolded Judge Blaisdell regarding an issue of integrity. Blaisdell refused to remove himself from hearing the case at the preliminary hearing. Jennings argued, correctly, that because Blaisdell heard the evidence at the inquest and at that time Lizzie Borden was a suspect and she was denied her right to counsel, he may be biased in his decisions and he should not preside over the hearing. In the Judge's response, in which he disagreed with Jennings, he stated that the inquest has nothing to do with the arraignment process so there was no conflict of interest. It is clear that Blaisdell's decision making was already biased against Lizzie Borden. No wonder at the completion of the preliminary hearing, on September 1, 1892, it is reported in most all covering newspapers that Judge Blaisdell found Lizzie A. Borden "probably guilty" and sent the case on to the grand jury for indictment.

On August 12, 1892, *The Woonsocket Call* reported:

> The Borden case at Fall River is apparently as much a mystery as ever, and apparently because the police are either incompetent or willfully stubborn…In the first place they made a grave mistake in not doing what every intelligent official should know enough to do at the start and that is, make a thorough examination of the premises.

Trial coverage of the Borden case was similar to that of the inquest, preliminary hearing, and the grand jury. In fact, with the grand jury proceeding, as discussed earlier, there would never have been an indictment if it were not for the testimony of Lizzie's close friend, Alice Russell. Each time a person testified at the trial, testimony was reported daily. It should be noted here that reporters back then used the term "trial" very loosely as they often referred to the preliminary hearing as her trial. But to avoid confusion, the preliminary hearing occurred in August 1892 and the actual trial was held in June 1893.

The strategy presented by the prosecution had six points: 1) motive, 2) predetermination, 3) opportunity, 4) actions, 5) lack of demonstrative guilt, and 6) lack of corroborated alibi. The strategy of the defense was simply to cross-examine the prosecution witnesses, whereby casting doubt or identifying testimony to show ambiguity in the prosecution's case. In their cross-examination, the defense presented alternatives to damaging testimony, pointed out conflicting statements, and questioned credibility of the state's witnesses. The defense had no burden to prove Lizzie's innocence because the burden automatically rested with the prosecution to prove her guilty. Printed news reports presented a synopsis of each witness that testified and the public was able to watch as the legend that was created during the previous nine months was shaken. The longer the trial continued, the more the media reported in favor of Lizzie. Some examples of reporting as the defense raised issues of credibility follow.

On June 9, 1893, *The New York Times* reported:

POLICE WITNESSES IN THE BORDEN
CASE DISAGREE

One witness swears that he saw the piece of Hatchet Handle alleged to be missing in the very box where the hatchet was found—If he did the Prosecution's theory of the murders fails in an important respect—a momentous question to be decided.

...they nearly destroyed the Government's hope of producing the instrument with which the deed was done and nearly, if not completely, disposed of the last hatchet which had been brought forward as the instrument which took the lives of Andrew Borden and his wife.

On June 9, 1893, *The Boston Daily Globe* reported:

The tattered web which the legal spiders for the Commonwealth have been weaving around her had one of its strongest threads snapped by a sudden and totally unexpected blow that left it sagging at one side. The Government's witnesses did not agree. One stuck to the outlined programme in his testimony and another followed him with a startling disclosure. Then the first witness was brought back and made to confirm his apparent insincerity.

On June 9, 1893, headlines of *The New York Times* reported:

NEW LIGHT
BIG SENSATION IN BORDEN CASE
OFFICER FLEET GETS
SADLY TWISTED
DID NOT MENTION ALL HE FIRST FOUND.
Mullaly (officer) Contradicts Fleet's story.
Says Hatchet Handle was in Box.

It is clear that by the closing of the prosecution that questions were raised regarding the competence of the investigation as well as the integrity of the investigators.

News reports contributed to another prosecutor mishap when a report of a police matron surfaced that indicated she overheard a conversation between Lizzie and Emma Borden while Lizzie was incarcerated. Hannah Regan told reporters or was *encouraged* to tell reporters that she overheard a conversation between Lizzie and Emma, in which Lizzie made incriminating statements. This report was later unfounded.

Syndicated columnist Joe Howard reported that on June 14, 1893, the following is an accurate synopsis of information provided by police matron Hannah Regan:

> I was standing in the closet, not more than four feet away when Lizzie said to her sister, "so you have given me away, haven't you?" To which Emma replied, "No I haven't" and Lizzie, measuring the end of her fore-finger with her thumb, said "Well, I won't give in that much."

However, during testimony at the trial, Howard's column reported that Regan testified briefly for the prosecution that this conversation occurred. Then Jennings cross-examined Regan on the issue that after she reported this incident she signed a paper and told witnesses that what she heard was a lie. Regan admitted she could not recall signing the paper or confessing to a lie. Jennings successfully halted that matter of testimony and raised yet another question of credibility upon a state's witness.

As a result of this combined carnival of events, Lizzie was acquitted. The jury, who was an all-white male panel, deliberated a short while and concluded that she was not guilty. Yet this acquittal did not end the media frenzy that would ultimately mark her life. As in life, her death was also a media event. On June 2, 1927, Lizzie Borden died, leaving most of her estate to the Society for the Prevention of Cruelty to Animals. Nine days after her death, her sister Emma passed also. Knowlton commented the following as reported by the *Associated Press*:

> Hosea M. Knowlton, later attorney general for the state,
> it was revealed that he had said, while waiting for the
> jury's verdict, and again a few weeks before his death,
> that if he could have known what Andrew J. Borden had
> said to John V. Morse, in the long conversation that the
> two men had had the night before the murder, in which
> Lizzie had come home and gone to her room, he believed
> he could have convicted somebody of the murder.

This can be interpreted to mean that at the time of the trial up until the time of Knowlton's death that he knew Lizzie Borden was not the killer, yet he pursued her anyway, for the public sake (as indicated in his correspondence with the Attorney General). Morse was never fully investigated, questioned, or targeted as Lizzie had experienced, yet his testimony could be interpreted as more inflammatory than her testimony. If what Lizzie said was true, that she returned home the night before proceeding immediately to her room and she heard Morse and her father arguing, any reasonable person would be inclined to consider the possibility that what they discussed was of the utmost importance. Why, then, did the police not get this information from Morse? It seems the answer to be very simple—they did not ask him. After all, in their minds they already had the killer and it was Lizzie, therefore, nothing further about any other witness mattered quite as much. They used their *expertise* to prosecute Lizzie Borden because she had no high regard for her stepmother.

Lizzie Borden was buried next to her father and her stepmother in the Oak Grove Cemetery, Fall River, Massachusetts. Emma died nine days later after a long illness. Much of the mystery that still surrounds this case has been lost forever with the deaths of so many of the people involved. These news reports situate the context in which Edwin Porter wrote *A Fall River Tragedy* which is discussed in the following essay. But before reading further, a few comments on the theoretical framework of Hans-Georg Gadamer on historicity and historically-effected consciousness integrated with Paul Ricoeur's historical consciousness help us to understand why a book published by a former reporter at the time of the investigation and trial had significant impact upon opinions and rumors and most of the local vernacular topics of the day.

HISTORICITY

Historicity invites "sensus communis" (Gadamer, 2002, p. 19), a term referring to common sense related to one's tradition and one's community. Historicity means that in our interpretative actions we listen to common sense questions of a particular time, not necessarily our own time period. This permits us to be driven by the ideas within the context rather than by our own agency. According to Gadamer (2002), historicity is a structure of understanding that is foreground in prejudice that gives us a beginning within a particular tradition, paying attention to a particular historical moment and permitting the traditions of that historical moment to live. This framework allows one to stand within history and not above history, which enables relevant and more accurate interpretative outcomes. Historicity permits and creates a historically-effected consciousness.

HISTORICALLY-EFFECTED CONSCIOUSNESS

The "historically-effected consciousness" (Gadamer, 2002, p. 341) integrates knowledge and effect. A historical consciousness takes on a reflective posture toward its own bias and the tradition and context in which it is situated (Gadamer, 2002). This means that one's interpretation of events is not only impacted by its own interpretive criteria but it is also impacted by its own situatedness—no longer naively assimilating into a new tradition and no longer impacted by one's own personal bias. The integrative reflection of both aspects governs interpretation and dissuades misinterpretation. The historically-effected consciousness is not just inquiry into tradition but it is a consciousness of work itself and therefore it has an effect on something or someone. Quite like Paul Ricoeur's (1988) "hermeneutics of historical consciousness" (p. 220), knowledge and effect is integrated, causing tensions between the past and present that aid in interpretive understanding. Ricoeur (1988) states:

> The past is revealed to us through the projection of a historical horizon that is both detached from the horizon of the present and taken up into and fused with it. This idea of a temporal horizon as something that is both projected and separate, distinguished and included,

brings about the dialectizing of the idea of traditionality.
(p. 220-221)

In other words, interpretive possibilities happen through our historically effected consciousness when the past and the present have import to the interpretive context. We cannot forget the past in our interpretive mode, yet we can also not forget the present as well, both must interplay with each other as we continue to examine and learn from those before us. Considering the notion of historicity, the historically-effected consciousness, and our historical consciousness, the possibilities of learning from our past is amplified and less subject to limitations. These ideas must be remembered as we read the following essay and consider the artifact as an artifact within the historical consciousness of the Borden case. The following essay was published in *The Hatchet: Journal of Lizzie Borden Studies*[2] and helps us to negotiate the philosophical hermeneutics of Gadamer and Ricoeur by way of a notorious case of murder and lies.

---

[2] Holba, A. (2005). Edwin Porter's Fall River tragedy: A hermeneutic entrance into the Borden mystery. *The Hatchet: Journal of Lizzie Borden Studies.* 2(6), 6–12.

REFERENCES

Gadamer, H. G. (2002). *Truth and method*. New York: Continuum.

Ricoeur, P. (1988). *Time and narrative*. vol. 3. Chicago: University of Chicago Press.

EDWIN PORTER'S *FALL RIVER TRAGEDY*:
A HERMENEUTIC ENTRANCE INTO THE BORDEN MYSTERY

It is a fact that numerous journalists covered the aftermath of the Borden murders on a fairly consistent basis. David Kent, in his *Lizzie Borden Sourcebook,* comments that the courtroom was packed beyond capacity and fifty more seats were added for members of the press as it became evident that newspaper reporters had taken an immense interest in the trial. Kent identifies Edwin Porter, a local reporter from the staff of the *Fall River Globe*, as one of the journalists assigned to the Borden trial (Kent, p. 322). One of Porter's main assignments was to cover police/crime news. As a result of Porter's assignment to the Borden trial, he published *The Fall River Tragedy: History of the Borden Murders* in 1893. Porter's account is written much like the journalistic style of the day that contained a complete narrative account of the case in a presentation that "makes a devastating case for Lizzie's guilt" (Williams, Smithburn, Peterson, p. 269).

The first half of the book explains events prior to the trial; the other half deals directly with the trial itself, day by day. Porter was given notice by attorney Jennings not to publish/release the book before the Borden trial because it could prejudice the case, and Porter was forbidden to print certain pictures or likenesses upon threat of injunction and legal proceedings (Rebello, p. 359). Sources tell us that even Lizzie herself did not care for the account of her circumstances in the book, so after her acquittal she purchased the pressing and destroyed as many copies of the book as she could find, although she was not able to destroy every one. In fact, in the Foreword of the 1985 reprint of Porter's text, Robert Flynn revealed that after a forty-year search, he located a copy of the original publication at which time he proceeded with the 1985 reprint. He believed that offering the reprint of the rare text would be important to those interested in the Fall River mystery. While Porter's text contains factual flaws and factoids, it also provides the audience with unique insight into the particular historical moment in which it was fashioned.

This essay argues that we can take a new look at the Porter text and find gems of wisdom that illuminate human experience in a world seemingly far removed from the one in which we reside. By considering a few of Porter's interesting factual flaws and factoids, we may be pointed towards a new insight into a different historical moment[3] and the renewed valuation of a dubious text.

The methodology of this essay explores Porter's text through a constructive hermeneutic approach that means the process begins by deconstructing the factual flaws and factoids followed by reconstruction of meaning. Edwin Porter created an account of the Borden case that has contributed to our understanding of Victorian New England through conceptualizations of gender, media, and the interplay between public and private spheres. By exploring *The Fall River Tragedy* through a constructive hermeneutic, serendipitous and novel meaning is illuminated which invites a new perspective into a story that has remained a significant point of interest in the historical American consciousness. This exploration begins by deconstructing factual flaws from the Porter text.

FACTUAL FLAWS

A fact is information that is presented as an event or evidence that is consistent with an actual occurrence. *The Fall River Tragedy* is a text pervaded by a display of information presented as facts but are not based on an actual occurrence. For the purpose of this essay, facts that are not based on factual occurrence are factual flaws. This author does not suggest that Edwin Porter was intentionally misrepresenting information; rather it is more likely that the book was written and published quickly to capitalize on the public's intense interest in the case. Nevertheless, page after page contains questions of accuracy as these "facts" are presented. For example, Porter stated, "Bridget was in her own room in the attic where she had gone to wash the windows" (p. 9). This statement is a factual flaw because it is not consistent with the trial testimony of Bridget Sullivan that is accepted as an actual occurrence. In the trial, Bridget testified that she went upstairs after washing the windows and after Andrew Borden returned home in the morning and rested in her room:

---

[3] This interests me because I find that as I teach university students they tend to seek to understand the past through a contemporary frame in which they have a personal connection. The problem with seeking to understand something from the past by standing above the event, we misinterpret and misunderstand the event itself. This misinterpretation reflects lost meaning.

Q. What did you do when you got to your bedroom?

A. I went up stairs to my bedroom. When I got up in the bedroom I laid in the bed.

The fact that Porter misrepresents the actions of Bridget is not as inflammatory as it is potentially just a sloppy mistake made by a reporter failing to compare his earlier reporting with what was later revealed in sworn testimony.

Another factual flaw concerns Porter's description of the front staircase in the Borden house. Porter stated, "Reaching a landing half way up where their eyes were on a level with the floor, they looked across the hall, through an open door, under the bed, and saw the prostrate form of the dead woman [Abby Borden]" (p. 10). While it is true that the first time Mrs. Borden's body is observed it is by a witness standing on the front staircase about half way up, there is a question as to whether or not there is an actual landing there. The staircase turns and steps are constructed to adjust to the direction of the hallway, thus the "landing" is a few steps that are constructed wider and in a more triangular shape as compared to the traditional width and shape of the first seven (approximate) steps in the whole staircase. While this might be a case for semantic consideration, it does represent that Porter's description is not a carefully crafted report of the crime scene. Bridget Sullivan's trial testimony does not indicate a "landing":

A. As I went up stairs I saw the body under the bed. I ran right into the room and stood at the foot of the bed.

Q. How far up stairs did you go before you saw the body?

A. I don't remember how far, but I remember to see the woman's clothing.

Q. What?

A. I don't remember how far up I went. I guess I went far enough to see.

The dictionary definition of "landing" is "a level part of a staircase (as at the end of a flight of stairs)."[4] We could argue semantics over whether

---

[4] Merriam-Webster's Collegiate Dictionary, 10th ed., p. 654.

or not the few steps in the staircase reflect a landing, but the point over the factual representation is established regardless of semantic theory. Porter's account is potentially an embellishment of the scene description that might serve more to provide vivid imagery as one tries to capture the scene itself if one has never entered the Borden home.

Another factual flaw is Porter's description of Andrew Borden, including referring to him as being "highly esteemed, retired from active life, without a known enemy" (p. 13). Porter's description of Andrew is an angelic representation that has been rebutted by witness interviews and Borden scholars (Rebello, p. 25-27). At the time *The Fall River Tragedy* was written, this representation could be indicative of a bias in Porter's perception of the victim, but not factual. Often, lives of victims of violent crime are presented though a "halo effect" (Devito, p. 97) out of respect for the dead or victimized, rather than out of a truth. These three small examples of factual flaws may seem unimportant in the overall scheme of the Borden story; however, Porter's book contains many such subtle flaws that can color our understanding of the account. In truth, these factual flaws guide how we come to interpret and understand the event, and may sometimes create factoids in popular culture.

FACTOIDS

A factoid is "an invented fact believed to be true because of its appearance in print."[5] The myriad of newspaper articles claiming to represent the case from official or unofficial sources resulted in the invasion of many factoids into the minds of those who were interested in following the case. Porter recounts Lizzie's initial questioning, "The conversation was prolonged and during the entire time Miss Lizzie controlled her emotions wonderfully for a young lady who had so recently been called upon to witness the blood of her father and step-mother flowing from dozens of hideous wounds" (p. 12). Besides other accounts that suggest Lizzie was not an emotional person, the factoid here suggests that Lizzie controlled her emotions (stoically) which might lead readers to believe Lizzie was a naturally emotional woman, which actually had not been established. Additionally, this factoid is connected to the factual flaw that assumes

---

[5] Merriam-Webster's Collegiate Dictionary, 10th ed., p. 416.

Lizzie saw her stepmother dead when she did not. The numerous news reports indicated so many different tales about Lizzie's experiences that finding the truth became difficult. Accepting the factoid was much easier than critically evaluating all the sources later.

Another factoid in *The Fall River Tragedy* suggested that the position that Andrew Borden was found in was a normal and comfortable position customary to his daily practices. Porter quoted Dr. Bowen as saying, "It was his custom to lie in that way. His position was perfectly natural" (p. 16). It is unclear in Porter's account if Bowen truly had the knowledge of how Andrew Borden liked to rest or repose; nevertheless, the language Porter uses as a quote from Bowen asserts this statement as fact, not as opinion. There is no basis for Porter at this point in the book to suggest that Bowen knew this as fact.

A third factoid suggested that money was the motive for the murders. Porter reports the words of Hiram Harrington, Andrew Borden's brother-in-law, "The trouble about money matters did not diminish, nor the acerbity of the family ruptures lessen" (p. 25). Additionally, Porter repeats Harrington is "positive that Emma knows nothing of the murder" (p. 26). In this case, Porter reflects opinion and conjecture—not facts, but in time these statements came to be factoid shaping our perception of the Borden mystery.

NEW PERSPECTIVES

From this short deconstruction of Porter's text we can come to the quick conclusion that *The Fall River Tragedy* is not a text worth reading if one wants to learn about the Borden murders and the aftermath from a factual perspective. For the imaginative readers seeking to find a gem of invention from which to make a dramatic account, this text might prove useful. The real value that this text holds is not so much connected to Lizzie Borden directly; rather, we gain new insight and a fresh perspective when we read between the factual flaws and factoids. What emerges is the revelation of a historical moment. From this we find evidence that offers cultural insight and new historical perspectives related to gender construction, media, and the interplay between public and private spheres in Victorian New England.

GENDER

While Porter often alluded to the guilt of Lizzie, from his accounts we can also understand Lizzie Borden to be a good citizen from a Greek philosophical perspective advanced by Isocrates. According to Isocrates, a good citizen is someone who acts as an embedded agent in the polis— the center of Greek life—market place/politics (Isocrates, 1928/1945; Poulakos, 1997). This person will be an individual who is guided by ethics and who has concern for the well being of the polis. While Isocrates may not have considered a woman to be a citizen, the other attributes of being a political agent, speaking for, in, and among others in the polis is a central requirement. Porter suggested Lizzie Borden was an embedded agent within the town of Fall River, at least as much as a woman could have been in her time. Before the murders, Porter reports that Lizzie "taught a class of young people [at her church]," was active in church work, and "was a member of the Fruit and Flower Mission and other charitable organizations as well as the Woman's Christian Temperance Union. In all of these she was considered a valuable and conscientious worker" (p. 23). Women had limited opportunity in the Victorian era. Lizzie stepped outside of her private realm and into the public realm in a capacity for service to her world (polis), potentially as an embedded agent. Without Porter's *Fall River Tragedy*, it is unlikely that we would immediately consider Lizzie Borden an ideal Greek citizen. Reading Porter's text through a constructive hermeneutic approach invites new possibilities for the reader to consider. To take an accused killer and see her through a rhetorical lens is a novel way of looking at the actors in this dramatic story. Through a constructive hermeneutic we can also take a glimpse of the media situated in the historical moment.

MEDIA

Edwin Porter's *The Fall River Tragedy* gives us insight into Victorian era media. By stating that "almost every newspaper in the country failed to accept it [referring to the Eli Bence incident] as authentic, and while it served to point the police toward a possible solution of the great murder mystery, it also brought down upon them the vituperation of many a bucolic newspaper man who knew not of what he wrote, or knowing cared little for justice and truth" (p. 20). Porter is highly critical of negligent news reports that apparently had become customary in the day. Porter also reports that a clergy member beckons to reporters writing on the crime to be "careful of the reputations of the living, which could so easily be undermined" (p. 42).

The accuracy of news reporting of the accounts from witnesses are exacerbated, as on the first day of the trial thirty-five reporters were present in the courtroom and only a few intimate friends were present for Lizzie (p. 158). While the audience changed during the trial, the media blitz also increased. Through this constructive hermeneutic, we also find a glimpse of public/private interplay in the culture of Victorian New England.

Public/Private Interplay

Porter suggested Lizzie did not act according to public norms for women in her time. Porter states that a police officer remarked that Lizzie "did not appear to be in the least bit excited or worried. I have wondered why she did not faint upon her discovery of the dead body of her father. Most women would have done so" (p. 28). By this, Porter implicitly suggested women have an appropriate way to behave in the public sphere as a sociocultural norm.

Porter also pointed to poor police procedure during the time as he suggested their mistakes were "not surprising" (p. 48). While the crime scene was not initially secured, Porter stated police were victims caught at a disadvantage because of the lack of available officers on duty (the rest were at a police social function); they were not available in the public realm. In fact, Porter suggested that if the police were more publicly available that there still would have been criticism directed at them by the citizens of Fall River (p. 48). This suggests that the public was just as critical and concerned over police issues in the Victorian era in New England as people are today.

The last insight into Victorian cultural norms pertains to the private realm of citizens. Porter reports that common folk had "intense excite-ment" (p. 52) about the case, as it was rather unique from most other daily happenings. Tensions increased and people became obsessed about organizing their daily tasks around either attending official proceedings or waiting for the next news report. Porter claimed people became focused on murder and "the community had reached a point when it felt that it must clear up the mystery or go insane" (p. 53). The most public event of a murder in a Massachusetts town had become the focus of most private lives of common citizens in Fall River. Society became obsessed as murder invaded their dreams, thus demonstrating a blurring of public and private realms of experience. We see this same manifestation connected to the recent catastrophic events since the new year (2005) as the tsunami invaded parts of Asia and now with the recent hurricanes and floods. People are hooked to electronic media, such as the Internet and cable television, much like people during the time of the Borden trial, waiting for the next news report to print and circulate. It seems human beings have the natural capacity to know when something different or new happens within a community. Because of this often-intuitive capacity, our engagement in the public and private sphere has the potential to transform experience in a community and allow the behavioral borders of public and private to overlap each other. We often think that we have come a long way since the Victorian era, but examining texts rhetorically through a constructive hermeneutic approach can remind us exactly how far we have come, or not.

CONCLUSION

This has been an attempt to find value in a historical work that has often been subjected to criticism. This essay argues that we can use Edwin Porter's *The Fall River Tragedy: A History of the Borden Murders* as a constructive hermeneutic entrance into American myth and culture, instead of critiquing the text to the point of complete devaluation. This exploration seeks to resurrect this text for future critical inquiry into the nature of the Borden mystery and of humankind.

References

DeVito, J.A. (2004) *The Interpersonal Communication Book*. Boston: Allyn and Bacon.

Flynn, R. (1985) Foreword. In Edwin Porter, *The Fall River tragedy: A history of the Borden murders*. Portland, ME: King Philip Publishing Co.

Isocrates. (1928/1945). *Isocrates*. 3 vols. Trans. George Norlin (vol. 1–2) and LaRue VanHook (vol. 3). London: William Heinemann.

Kent, D. (1992). *The Lizzie Borden Sourcebook*. Boston: Branden Publishing Company, Inc.

Merriam-Webster's Collegiate Dictionary (1993). 10th ed. Springfield, MA: Merriam-Webster, Inc.

Porter, E.H. (1893). *The Fall River Tragedy: A History of the Borden Murders*. Portland, ME: King Philip Publishing Co.

Poulakos, T. (1997). *Speaking for the polis: Isocrates rhetorical education*. Columbia, SC: University of South Carolina Press.

Rebello, L. (1999). *Lizzie Borden past & present: A comprehensive reference to the life and times of Lizzie Borden*. Fall River, MA: Al-Zach Press.

Williams, J.G., Smithburn, J.E., Peterson, M.J. (Eds.) (1980). *Lizzie Borden: A case book of family and crime in the 1890s*. Bloomington, IN: T.I.S. Publishing.

QUESTIONS FOR DISCUSSION
ON CHAPTER 3

1. Define historicity in your own words.
2. Define historically-effected consciousness in your own words.
3. What is the relationship between historicity and historically-effected consciousness?
4. Define factoid.
5. Can you think of other contemporary cases where the issue of historicity has come into the discussion?
6. What other recent public/political situations involve issues of historical consciousness?
7. Take a current events issue and explore the notion of historicity and historically-effected consciousness. How different or similar are these scenarios?

CHAPTER 4

FROM LIZZIE TO LIZBETH: WHAT'S IN A NAME?

Are names rhetorical? According to Roderick Hart (1990), rhetoric has six functions which include: 1) it unburdens, 2) it distracts, 3) it enlarges, 4) it names, 5) it empowers, and 6) it elongates. The function that concerns this chapter is the rhetorical function of naming something. The act of naming or renaming something provides a type of identification or re-identification for the subject—to either connect or disconnect to something else. The act of naming helps listeners become acquainted with and/or more comfortable with ideas, people, or events so that understanding can be achieved. The act of naming also gives us a vocabulary so that we can communicate about something to someone else with potential for understanding, agreement, disagreement, or to begin to cultivate common ground.

When we name something, we define it. This act of definition provides order and clarity—it is a poetic method (Burke, 1984). A name is a form that sets up anticipation—the act of calling out one's name implies a desire to hear a response. There is relief when we hear that response because that response acknowledges the other in a way that is meaningful and life-affirming (Hyde, 2006). These notions can help us consider Lizzie's name change as a symbolic and rhetorical act. This chapter examines Lizzie Borden's name change from Lizzie Andrew Borden as her birth name to Lizbeth Borden, which she took after her acquittal. While several works of fiction attempt to explain her name change in somewhat simplistic terms, this chapter considers four possibilities that led to her name change; they include 1) her name change as a "linguistic covenant" (Weaver, 1970, p. 114); 2) her name change as a linguistic response to her emotions (Ellul, 1985); 3) her name change as a form of positive acknowledgment (Hyde, 2006); and finally, 4) her name change as a necessary catalyst for purge and catharsis (Burke, 1968). Richard Weaver (1970) argued that "rhetorical language, or language which would persuade, must always be particularized to suit the occasion" (p. 63). Acknowledging Weaver's claim, this analysis begins with the premise that the act of naming or renaming and the name itself is the engagement of rhetorical language that intends to persuade in a given situation. In the case of Lizzie's name change to Lizbeth, the act of the name change and the name selected itself intended to persuade somebody of something. Specifically and simply, the act of changing her name was her way of trying to persuade the public to see her differently, to escape from their memory of her trial. The name she chose adds rhetorical implications because it signifies one as a proper adult, quite the change from "Lizzie" which colloquially implies a child's name. This analysis begins with her name change as a linguistic covenant.

LINGUISTIC COVENANT

Richard Weaver (1970) was concerned with the relationship between words and the "extramental" order they symbolize (p. 114). "Meaning and value are closely bound" which allows us to see this relationship as a "linguistic covenant" (p. 114). The idea of a covenant is doubly symbolic because not only does it represent a particular word, it also represents a relationship between the word (signifier) and the signified. This relation-ship points toward an ethics of rhetoric that requires particular terms for engagement. The language we select to represent who we are as individuals should be ethically embedded within the particular situation so that communicative engagement can improve and become more effective. If we attend to this ethical embeddedness we become more likely to adhere to that linguistic covenant and shield us from "thoughtless rhetoric" (Weaver, 1970, p. 112). Lizzie's name change to Lizbeth was a type of linguistic covenant that she hoped would help her to re-identify with ethics of rhetoric within the Fall River community.

Lizzie-Lizbeth never moved out of Fall River but she did move, initially with her sister, Emma, to a better part of town where she thought she belonged. Growing up as a child and continuing on until immediately before her father's murder, the Borden family lived beneath their means. Lizzie-Lizbeth's name change was a type of linguistic covenant that would allow her to permit herself to be shielded from thoughtless rhetorics from within her own community. If she promised to be a lady, if she promised to grow up in a sense, she would be able to remain in Fall River despite the broken covenant that manifested as her father and stepmother's murder. The name change does not imply she was guilty, rather it implies that she wanted a chance to renew her damaged ethical ethos from her trial and acquittal for the murders of her father and step-mother. This linguistic covenant was not, however, without emotion.

LINGUISTIC RESPONSE

Jacques Ellul (1985) argues speech "involves emotions that transcend reflexes" (p. 3). The Lizzie-Lizbeth name change was also a linguistically emotional response. According to Ellul (1970), language is not just an utterance devoid of otherness and context, it overflows its limits; language goes beyond and restructures meaning, ambiguity, and variation in interpretation. Words evoke traces, echoes, and feelings intermingled with thoughts and reasons of irrationality, as well as motives and urges that are fleeting and uncoordinated. The concerns from Ellul suggest that there is more to the name itself—there is a beyondness that is contingent and slightly paradoxical, uncertain, and sometimes unforgiving. In a name change, this flux represents the choice that is made to change one's name—the choice that involves hope for a better and more certain future.

Lizzie-Lizbeth's name change was imbued with emotion. Her life leading up to the act of changing her name was full of the uncertainties and paradoxes that define irrationality. This name change was a way for Lizzie-Lizbeth to understand and come to terms with her experience. It caused her to consider and rethink her place in the world as she chose to rhetorically shift her emotions from a Lizzie connected to murder, specifically parricide, and the unwelcoming experience from her home for her whole life in Fall River. The rhetorical act of changing her name allowed her to find a welcome of sorts and bring the emotionality to a reasonable pace. Both the linguistic covenant and the linguistic response lead us to the next reason for the name change, the need for linguistic acknowledgment.

LINGUISTIC ACKNOWLEDGMENT

Michael Hyde (2006) argues that acknowledgment provides a way of responding to distressful situations because it is a communicative behavior that attends to the other in a way that makes room for them in the world and in our lives. Lizzie-Lizbeth was seeking this linguistic acknowledgment which she had always and previously known in Fall River, MA. Linguistic acknowledgment is powerful as it can give one a reason to want to exist at a time when the one questions her or his well being or self-worth. Linguistic acknowledgment permits one to feel at home physically, emotionally, and even spiritually.

After Lizzie-Lizbeth's acquittal she did physically remain in her hometown but she did not achieve the acknowledgment that she previously had or legitimately needed. Lizzie-Lizbeth needed emotional and spiritual acknowledgment after the trial and at the realization of her father's death once all of the hype dissipated. Lizzie-Lizbeth did not have clear opportunity to legitimately grieve after the murders; the act of changing her name provided her an opportunity for linguistic acknowledgment—people could get to know her again, acknowledge her again, and she could then find her home, physically, emotionally, or spiritually. By changing her name she restructured or rearticulated the organization of her embodiment in order to seek acknowledgment from her peers and other community members. Acknowledgment is life-giving (Hyde, 2006) as it can give life to an otherwise lifeless existence. Part of this life is the biological necessity of purge and catharsis. We need this biological function in order to exist.

PURGE AND CATHARSIS

Kenneth Burke's (1968) theory of form is based upon the notion of purge and catharsis. Aristotle's (antiquity/ 1984) notion of tragedy implies the need to be cleansed of emotional tensions in a deliberate fashion. Burke takes this notion of tragedy and suggests it is directly related to a predictable communicative form that gives life to the human agent through the need to purge and the catharsis or transformative cleansing that results. Burke's theory of form is a poetic process in that it is favorable for a gradual rise to a crisis and a climax or crescendo that leads to a release or often a cleansing that provides an experience of catharsis. In this process the form of the event or linguistic act makes the audience or rhetor anticipate something. Form itself is the creation of an appetite in the mind of the auditor and attention is given to pleasing that appetite. There are set backs and frustrations that create tension and dissonance until the point where resolution is achieved—this resolution often comes with a catharsis-driven act.

The name change from Lizzie to Lizbeth represents that poetic process that led Lizzie-Lizbeth to purge and transform in the aftermath of the Borden tragedy. Burke (1984) argued that the purpose of the poetic process is a social purpose intended to unite socially. Lizzie's name change to Lizbeth is an example of that poetic process because she sought a social purpose. Lizzie-Lizbeth did not need friends in Fall River nor did she want her existence to return to her previous mode of existence before the murders; nevertheless, Lizzie-Lizbeth did want that feeling of home, after all, she chose not to move away from Fall River, it had been her childhood home and she was certain to remain there. The poetic process of changing her name allowed her to make an attempt to bridge the gap between herself and the community. It allowed her to try to unite socially and find herself situated and finally back home. Whether Lizzie-Lizbeth ever really felt at home, felt linguistic acknowledgment, or adhered to her linguistic covenant, she did find that internal purge and catharsis enabled her to revision herself before the Fall River community. While Lizzie-Lizbeth did everything she could have done to be reunited socially, the decision ultimately ended up with her audience who proved to be tougher than most expected. Of course with the passing of time, Lizzie-

Lizbeth has found a home posthumously. Lizzie-Lizbeth is the narrative that identifies Fall River, Massachusetts. Lizzie-Lizbeth gets more visitors at her house and final resting place now more than ever during her lifetime, and Lizzie-Lizbeth has become a role model for oppressed and victimized women. While the name change may not have given Lizzie-Lizbeth the total catharsis she needed at the time, her memory and spirit certainly have achieved it today.

CONCLUSION

Language as symbolic action (Burke, 1966) helps us to resonate with understanding why Lizzie changed her name to Lizbeth. Action involves character and choice. Action implies the ethical embedded within the human personality (Burke, 1970). Lizzie-Lizbeth Borden changed her name because of the ethical; she wanted to re-create a linguistic covenant because the murders severed any covenant previously existing; she wanted to make an emotional linguistic response to a devastating situation in her life; she wanted to find linguistic acknowledgment within her newly defined existence after her acquittal; and finally and most importantly, Lizzie-Lizbeth wanted to experience a purging and catharsis after her ordeal. This cleansing was paramount to her continued existence in Fall River, as it was her ethical choice to remain in the community that reminded her so much of very dark times. Lizzie did not change her name to announce to the world her sexual orientation; she did not change her name to announce to the world that she was an independent woman; she did not change her name to announce to the world that she grew up. Lizbeth Borden changed her name because she, like all human agents, was a symbol-using animal who rhetorically and linguistically existed first before her physical existence. The rhetorical and linguistic existence ensure her physical existence and Lizbeth was doing just that, assuring her physical existence by recognizing the need to exist rhetorically and linguistically.

REFERENCES

Aristotle. (antiquity/ 1984). *Poetics*. In E. Corbett (Ed). *The Rhetoric and poetics of Aristotle*. New York: Modern Library.

Burke, K. (1984). *Permanence and change*. Berkeley: University of California Press.

Burke, K. (1970). *The rhetoric of religion: Studies in logology*. Berkeley: University of California Press.

Burke, K. (1968). *Counter-statement*. Berkeley: University of California Press.

Burke, K. (1966). *Language as symbolic action: Essays on life, literature, and method*. Berkeley: University of California Press

Ellul, J. (1985). *The humiliation of the word*. Grand Rapids, MI: William B. Eerdmans Publishing.

Hart, R. (1990). *Modern rhetorical criticism*. Glenville, IL: Scott Foresman.

Hyde, M. (2006). *The life-giving gift of acknowledgment*. West Lafayette, IN: Purdue University Press.

Weaver, R. M. (1970). *Language is sermonic: Richard M. Weaver on the nature of rhetoric*. Baton Rouge, LA: Louisana State Unviersity Press.

QUESTIONS FOR DISCUSSION
ON CHAPTER 4

1. Describe Richard Weaver's linguistic covenant as it relates to a name change.
2. Describe Jacque Ellul's linguistic response as it relates to a name change.
3. Describe Michael Hyde's linguistic acknowledgment as it relates to a name change.
4. Consider contemporary name changes. Explain the rhetorical implications of celebrity name changes. Also, consider the name changes that drop last or first names, such as the following:

> Oprah (television personality)
> Ellen (television personality)
> Martha (television personality)
> Kennedy (Nigel Kennedy–classical/jazz violinist)

CHAPTER 5

FORENSIC ANALYSIS
AND RHETORICAL DISCREPANCIES

An inquest is a legal proceeding that occurs in a courtroom but in essence is an investigative tool utilized by the District Attorney to find evidence of a crime. The inquest began on Tuesday, August 9, 1892, just five days after the murders. It lasted three days and Lizzie testified each day, along with a select few other witnesses. There are numerous issues raised upon examination of the inquest in this matter. The issues include: 1) the District Attorney knowingly questioned Lizzie as his main suspect and denied her right to counsel by failing to advise her of that right, 2) the DA badgered the witness, 3) frustration mounted upon the District Attorney, 4) the DA's failure to follow through with appropriate investigatory questions, and finally 5) the *myth* of Lizzie's *inconsistent* testimony or, as Knowlton described it, her *confession*. Utilizing Lizzie's inquest testimony, we can examine these issues specifically.

Often inquests are held due to insufficient evidence to charge anyone with the deaths, which was the case with the Borden murders. Instead of the police conducting an unbiased investigation, they hoped to trick Lizzie into confessing the crime. When Lizzie was ordered to the inquest, Knowlton had an arrest warrant for her, signed and ready to be executed. But there was not enough evidence to support that warrant; therefore, he needed to try to obtain additional evidence from the inquest. It was Judge Blaisdell's duty to inform Lizzie of her right to counsel but his excuse in not doing so was that he thought her attorney, Jennings, already informed her. This mistake should never have occurred. All of the officials involved had many years of professional experience and a mistake this large simply should not have been acceptable. This, in fact, was a denial of Lizzie's rights afforded to her under Massachusetts State law that had a protection clause similar to Miranda v. Arizona (1966) as we know it today (Brown, 1991).

An obvious questionable inquest issue is that of Lizzie's inconsistent testimony. Examiners of the inquest transcript suggest Lizzie lied when she answered questions regarding Morse's habit of visiting the Borden residence, about her whereabouts when Andrew came home the morning of the murders, and her whereabouts during the morning of the murders. I argue that Lizzie did not lie at this proceeding but was still under the influence of morphine and somewhat confused about details. Apparently, after the discovery of the murders, Dr. Bowen began to sedate Lizzie due to the trauma of discovering her father murdered. At the trial, defense counsel cross examined Dr. Bowen relative to this issue:

Q. Did you have occasion to prescribe for her on account of this mental distress and nervous excitement, after that?
A. Yes sir.
Q. When was it?
A. Friday.
Q. Was the prescription or medicine the same as the other?
A. It was different.
Q. What was it?
A. Sulphate of morphine.
Q. In what doses?
A. One eighth of a grain.
Q. When?
A. Friday night at bedtime.
Q. The next day you changed that?
A. I did not change the medicine but doubled the dose.
Q. That was on Saturday?
A. On Saturday.
Q. Did you continue the dose on Sunday?
A. Yes sir.

Q. Did you continue it on Monday?
A. Yes sir.
Q. And on Tuesday?
A. Yes sir.
Q. How long did she continue to have that?
A. She continued to have that all the time she was in the station house.
Q. After her arrest, was it not?
A. And before.
Q. In other words, she had it all the time up to the time of her arrest, the hearing and while in the station house?
A. Yes sir.
Q. Does not morphine, given in double doses to allay mental distress and nervous excitement, somewhat affect the memory and change and alter the view of things and give people hallucinations?
A. Yes sir. (Kent, 1992a, p. 109)[1]

This confirms the heavy dosage of morphine that Lizzie had been given, and it demonstrates she was still under its influence at her inquest proceeding. Therefore, the following areas of *inconsistent* testimony are more likely the result of her being drugged rather than lying.

From the inquest testimony there were several areas that Lizzie did not provide precise answers. When Knowlton questioned Lizzie regarding coming downstairs the morning of the murders, he asked Lizzie about her conversation with Bridget:

Q. Tell us again what time you came downstairs.
A. It was a little before nine, I should say. About quarter. I don't know sure…
Q. Did you say anything to Maggie?
A. I did not.
Q. Did you say anything about washing the windows?
A. No sir.

---

[1] All inquest testimony is taken from the transcript included in the following text: Kent, D. (1992). *Lizzie Borden sourcebook*. Boston: Branden Publishing Company, Inc.

Q. Did you speak to her?

A. I think I told her I did not want any breakfast.

Q. You do not remember about talking about washing the windows?

A. I don't remember whether I did or not. I don't remember it. Yes, I remember. Yes, I asked her to shut the parlor blinds when she got through because the sun was so hot.

Knowing Lizzie had been under so much influence of morphine, her answers seem only appropriate. There should be more concern if her answers had been rehearsed, prepared, and memorized, while the prosecution might suggest that she lied when she testified about her whereabouts when her father left and returned home that morning. Let's let the testimony speak for itself:

Q. How long was your father gone?

A. I don't know that.

Q. Where were you when he returned?

A. I was down in the kitchen.

Q. What doing?

A. Reading an old magazine that had been left in the cupboard, and old Harper's magazine.

Q. Had you got through ironing?

A. No sir.

Q. Had you stopped ironing?

A. Stopped for the flats.

Q. Were you waiting for them to be hot?

A. Yes sir.

Q. Was there a fire in the stove?

A. Yes sir.

Q. When your father went away, you were ironing then?

A. I had not commenced, but was getting the little ironing board and the flannel.

Q. Are you sure you were in the kitchen when your father returned?

A. I am not sure whether I was there or in the dining room.

Then the testimony modulated to whether Lizzie was upstairs or downstairs at the time Andrew returned.

Q. Did you spend any time up the front stairs before your father returned?

A. No sir.

Q. Or after he returned?

A. No sir. I did stay in my room long enough when I went up to sew a little piece of tape on a garment.

Q. Was that the time when your father came home?

A. He came home after I came downstairs.

Q. You were not upstairs when he came home?

A. I was not upstairs when he came home, no sir.

Q. What was Maggie doing when your father came home?

A. I don't remember whether she was there or whether she had gone upstairs. I can't remember.

Q. Who let your father in?

A. I think he came to the front door and rang the bell and I think Maggie let him in and he said he had forgotten his key. So I think she must have been downstairs…

Q. Where were you when the bell rang?

A. I think in my room upstairs.

Q. Then you were upstairs when your father came home?

A. I don't know sure, but I think so.

Q. What were you doing?

A. As I say, I took up these clean clothes and stopped and basted a little piece of tape on a garment.

Q. Did you come down before your father was let in?

A. I was on the stairs coming down when she let him in…

Q. You remember Miss Borden, I will call your attention to it so as to see if I have any misunderstanding, not for the purpose of confusing you, you remember that you told me several times that you were downstairs and not upstairs when your father came home? You have forgotten perhaps?

A. I don't know what I have said. I have answered so many questions and I am so confused I don't know one thing from

another. I am telling you just as nearly as I know…I think I
was downstairs in the kitchen.

Later, Knowlton questioned Lizzie in the same fashion regarding what
she had been doing in the barn at the time of the murders.

> Q. How long did you remain there?
> A. I don't know. Fifteen or twenty minutes.
> Q. What doing?
> A. Trying to find lead for a sinker.
> Q. What made you think there would be lead for a sinker up
>   there?
> A. Because there was some there.
> Q. Was there not some by the door?
> A. Some pieces of lead by the open door but there was a box full
>   of old things upstairs.
> Q. Did you bring any sinker back from the barn?
> A. Nothing but a piece of chip I picked up on the floor…
> Q. Had you got a fish line?
> A. Not here. We had some at the farm.
> Q. Had you got a fish hook?
> A. No sir.
> Q. Had you got any apparatus for fishing at all?
> A. Yes. Over there.
> Q. Had you any sinkers over there?
> A. I think there were some. It is so long since I have been there,
>   I think there were some.
> Q. You had no reason to suppose you were lacking sinkers?
> A. I don't think there were any on my lines.

This questioning continued until Knowlton became so frustrated, in trying
to show Lizzie as lying, he just appears to be frustrated with his lack of
listening skills.

> Q. It occurred to you after your father came in it would be a good
>   time to go to the barn after sinkers and you had no reason to

suppose there was not an abundance of sinkers at the farm and an abundance of lines?

A. The last time I was there, there were some lines.

Q. Did you not say before you presumed there were sinkers at the farm?

A. I don't think I said so.

Q. You did say so exactly. Do you now say you presume there were not sinkers at the farm?

A. I don't think there were any fishing lines suitable to use at the farm. I don't think there were any sinkers on any line that had been mine.

Q. Do you remember telling me you presumed there were lines and sinkers and hooks at the farm?

A. I said there were lines, I thought perhaps hooks. I did not say I thought there were sinkers on my lines. There was another box of lines over there beside mine.

Q. You thought there were not sinkers?

A. Not on my lines.

This demonstrated that while Lizzie might have seemed confused, she is not inconsistent. Lizzie did not change her story but she did clarify it. Knowlton heard her answers as he wanted to hear them, and he appeared to only hear what he believed he could use to confuse her. This only added to his frustrations. A few questions later, Knowlton's frustration projected:

Q. What was the use of telling me a while ago you had no sinkers on your line at the farm?

A. I thought I made you understand that those lines at the farm were no good to use.

Q. Did you not mean for me to understand one of the reasons you were searching for sinkers was that the lines you had at the farm, as you remembered then, had no sinkers on them?

A. I said the lines at the farm had no sinkers.

Q. I did not ask you what you said. Did you not mean for me to understand that?

A. I meant for you to understand I wanted the sinkers and was going to have new lines.

Another area of questioning where it is apparent that Knowlton was not carefully listening to Lizzie's answers occurred when he questioned her about what she did upstairs prior to Andrew's return home that morning. The second day of questioning, Knowlton inquired as to what Lizzie did that morning in question:

Q. You mean you went up there to sew a button on?
A. I basted a piece of tape on.
Q. Do you remember you did not say that yesterday?
A. I don't think you asked me. I told you yesterday I went upstairs directly after I came up from down cellar, with the clean clothes.

Lizzie was correct. On the first day of the testimony, Lizzie answered:

A. No sir. I did stay in my room long enough when I went up to sew a little piece of tape on a garment.

It was clear that Lizzie remembered this correctly. Knowlton wanted to hear something other than what Lizzie had to say. He was doing everything he could to confuse the issue and portray Lizzie as a liar. This same type of question and answer continued when Knowlton questioned Lizzie about her knowledge of Morse's visit.

Q. How many times this last year has he been at your house?
A. None at all to speak of. Nothing more than a night or two at a time.
Q. How often did he come to spend a night or two?
A. Really, I don't know. I am away so much myself.
Q. Your last answer is that you don't know how much he had been here because you had been away yourself so much?
A. Yes.
Q. That is true the last year or so since he has been east?

A. I have not been away the last year so much but other times I have been away when he has been here.

Q. Do I understand you to say that his last visit before this one was 14 years ago?

A. No. He has been here once between the two.

Q. How long did he stay then?

A. I don't know.

Q. How long ago was that?

A. I don't know.

The questioning continued in this fashion as Knowlton attempted to get Lizzie to answer the same question with a different answer to make her look as if she is lying. The ironic part is that he never really got anywhere with this line of questioning other than to make himself look like he has poor listening skills.

There were times in Knowlton's questioning that he did not follow through with the next logical question. This leads one to believe that either Knowlton did not want to pursue the issue or he did not see the issue. In asking Lizzie if she was aware of anyone who was on bad terms with her father, Knowlton did not pursue the answer offered:

Q. Besides that, do you know of anybody that your father had bad feelings toward or who had bad feelings toward your father?

A. I know of one man who has not been friendly with him. They have not been friendly for years.

Q. Who?

A. Mr. Hiram C. Harrington.

Q. What relation is he to him?

A. He is my father's brother-in-law.

Q. Your mother's brother?

A. My father's only sister married Mr. Harrington.

Q. Anybody else that was on bad terms with your father or that your father was on bad terms with?

A. Not that I know of.

Knowlton never followed through with asking why they were on bad terms, which seemed to be the next logical question. Later in testimony Lizzie described herself as having a difference of opinion with Abby over something about Abby's half sister, Mrs. George Whitehead. Knowlton never asked what the difference was about and possibly he did not think it related to these murders.

> Q. Did you ever have any trouble with your stepmother.
> A. No sir.
> Q. Have you within six months had any words with her?
> A. No sir.
> Q. Within a year?
> A. No sir.
> Q. Within two years?
> A. I think not.
> Q. When last that you know of?
> A. About five years ago.
> Q. What about?
> A. Her step sister, half sister.
> Q. What name?
> A. Her name now is Mrs. George Whitehead.
> Q. Nothing more than hard words?
> A. No sir. They were not hard words. It was simply a difference of opinion.
> Q. You have been on pleasant terms with your stepmother since then?
> A. Yes sir.

Knowlton continued to question Lizzie about the level of cordiality that existed between her and Abby, and again, never really makes a point. Knowlton failed to follow through on what the difference of opinion was about. This could have been directly related to a different motive for the crime but it is not addressed.

Another area where Knowlton did not follow through in his questioning was when Lizzie described Andrew as he returned home the day of his murder.

Q. When you did go into the sitting room to ask him a question, if it was the sitting room, what took place then?

A. I asked him if he had any mail. He said "None for you." He had a letter in his hand. I supposed it was for himself. I asked him how he felt. He said "About the same." He said he should lie down. I asked him if he thought he should have a nap. He said he should try to. I asked him if he wanted the window left the way it was or if he felt a draught. He said "No." That is all.

Q. Did you help him about lying down?

The questioning continued about how Andrew laid on the sofa but what is dropped from the line of questioning is the potential mail or white parcel that Andrew had in his hand. Lizzie was never asked what happened to the letter and nothing is later pursued about it. This could have been important to the identification of the murderer or provide information about the will that may or may not have existed.

At the end of Lizzie's testimony, Knowlton again cut her off because she was not attending to his line of questioning. Specifically, he almost pleads with her to give him information to help solve this case. Lizzie began to respond and Knowlton cut her off because he believed she was going to repeat something she said at the beginning of the inquest about a man that had words with Andrew at the house. But Lizzie had other information about seeing a stranger at her house and being frightened. Knowlton made light of this stranger and then asks her if she found out whom the stranger was (Kent, 1992b). This, however, is not the job for witnesses, but it is the responsibility of the police to determine. It should not have been Lizzie's responsibility to find out who the man was that was lurking in the dark at her residence. It is not as if he will come forward, especially if he is the killer. Knowlton cut her off and then inappropriately placed the responsibility on her when the criminal justice system places the burden of innocent or guilt on the prosecution, not the accused.

Lastly, Knowlton badgered Lizzie throughout her testimony. As he tried to confuse issues and call her a liar, he badgered her to the point where it is obvious that Knowlton thought this was his last opportunity to solve the murders. Instead, he appeared to be grasping at straws. A few examples follow:

> Q. Can you give me any explanation why all you have told me would occupy more than three minutes?
>
> A. Yes. It would take me more than three minutes.
>
> Q. To look in that box you have described the size of on the bench and put down the curtain and then get out as soon as you conveniently could; would you say you were occupied in that business 20 minutes?
>
> A. I think so because I did not look at the box when I first went up.
>
> Q. What did you do?
>
> A. I ate my pears.
>
> Q. Stood there eating the pears, doing nothing?
>
> A. I was looking out of the window.
>
> Q. Stood there looking out of the window, eating pears?
>
> A. I should think so.
>
> Q. How many did you eat?
>
> A. Three I think.
>
> Q. You were feeling better than you did in the morning?
>
> A. Better than I did the night before.
>
> Q. You were feeling better than you were in the morning?
>
> A. I felt better in the morning than I did the night before.
>
> Q. That is not what I asked you. You were then, when you were in that hay loft, looking out the window and eating three pears, feeling better, were you not, than you were in the morning when you could not eat any breakfast?
>
> A. I never eat breakfast.
>
> Q. You did not answer my question and you will, if I have to put it all day. Were you then when you were eating those three pears in that hot loft, looking out that closed window, feeling better than you were in the morning when you ate no breakfast?
>
> A. I was feeling well enough to eat the pears.
>
> Q. Were you feeling better than you were in the morning?

A. I don't know how to answer you because I told you I felt better in the morning anyway.

Q. Do you understand my question? My question is whether, when you were in the loft of the barn, you were feeling better than you were in the morning when you got up?

A. No, I felt about the same.

Q. Were you feeling better than you were when you told your mother you did not care for any dinner?

A. No sir. I felt about the same.

Q. Well enough to eat pears, but not well enough to eat anything for dinner?

A. She asked me if I wanted any meat.

Q. I ask you why you should select that place, which was the only place which would put you out of sight of the house, to eat those three pears in?

Questioning continued in this fashion. Knowlton did not achieve what he set out to achieve, a confession to the murders, by way of exploring how Lizzie could eat the pears in the barn and not want her dinner. He failed to make a point in favor of the prosecution.

In questioning Lizzie about hypothetical blood found on one of her skirts, Knowlton tried to confuse Lizzie or say something that he could use to twist her words, but Lizzie remained intact from this assault.

Q. Did you give the officer the same skirt you had on the day of the tragedy?

A. Yes sir.

Q. Do you know whether there was any blood on the skirt?

A. No sir.

Q. Assume that there was, do you know how it got there?

A. No sir.

Q. Have you any explanation of how it might come there?

A. No sir.

Q. Did you know there was any blood on that skirt you gave them?

A. No sir.

> Q. Assume that there was. Can you give any explanation of how it came there on the dress skirt?
> A. No sir.

Knowlton continued this line of questioning to no avail. People listening to the parade of questions may fail to see the illogic and be drafted on Knowlton's band wagon of the assault on Lizzie.

In the end, after three days of testimony, Judge Blaisdell found enough evidence to serve the warrant for her arrest, except they decided to prepare a new one based on her *confession* and *conflicting* statements. This is only the beginning of the parade of events that will remain in the public attention for the next nine months and provide the backdrop for the Lizzie legacy today.

PRELIMINARY HEARING, GRAND JURY, AND THE TRIAL

The next phase of the Borden case was the preliminary hearing. This hearing commenced three weeks after the crime and the purpose was to determine if there was probable cause to proceed on to the next criminal justice phase, which would be a formal indictment and then on to trial. The actual transcript of the preliminary hearing was initially sequestered and subsequently lost. Newspaper accounts were often inaccurate and therefore were not a good source for reliable information. Jennings' personal copy was found and is now on display with the Fall River Historical Society Museum. Since there was no official transcript to be examined, people relied upon the synopsis of testimony from the news reports and by word of mouth. This is one reason that there is so much false information leading to the legend of Lizzie Borden. Arnold Brown (1991), in his book *Lizzie Borden: The legend, the truth, the final chapter*, presents one example from the testimony of John Morse. Under cross-examination, Jennings asked:

> Q. Did you notice the at all the cellar door, whether it was open or shut?
> A. I think it was open; I won't say for sure, but I think it was.

Q. When you first went to the back of the house?
A. Yes sir.
Q. Wide open, or partly open?
A. Well, I could not say. (Brown, 1991, pp. 80-81)

It is clear that Morse wasn't really sure and had no clear recollection of the position of the door. On August 27, 1892, *The Fall River Globe* reported the exchange somewhat differently:

Q. Are you sure the cellar door was open? [Jennings]
A. I am sure. [Morse]

This is such a misleading representation of the actual testimony no wonder the legend of Lizzie Borden is so far removed from the truth. Another example comes from author Edgar Lustgarten (1950) in his book, *Verdict in Dispute*; his description of testimony states that Bridget found the front door not only locked but bolted, and she struggled to get it open so as not to keep Andrew waiting. Lustgarten (1950) tells us that somebody behind Bridget laughed out loud and that she glanced over her shoulder and saw Lizzie standing at the top of the staircase, a few feet from the open door of the guest room. Lustgarten represents the facts surrounding when Andrew returned home and Bridget had to let him in the locked door. He argues that Bridget actually saw Lizzie on the steps at the time of the laugh. In the actual trial testimony, that is not what Bridget says at all when questioned by Knowlton:

Q. Up until the time you had let Mr. Borden in, had you seen Miss Lizzie?
A. She was upstairs at the time I let him in.
Q. Where upstairs?
A. She might be in the hall, for I heard her laugh.
Q. At the time you let Mr. Borden in?
A. Yes sir.
Q. Was that the first time you had heard or seen her since you spoke to her at the back door?
A. Yes sir.

Q. You had not seen her or Mrs. Borden during the intermediate time?

A. No sir.

Q. What was the occasion of her laugh?

A. I got puzzled at the door, I said something, and she laughed at it; I supposed that must make her laugh-I don't know.

Q. Did she laugh out loud?

A. Yes sir.

Q. Say anything?

A. No sir.

Q. How soon did you see her?

A. It might be five or ten minutes after she came downstairs; she came through the front hall, I don't know whether she came from the upstairs. She came through the sitting room, I was in the sitting room.

The Lizzie legend says that Bridget saw her on the steps when she laughed. Authors like Lustgarten support this misinformation and so the myth of misinformation continues. It is apparent that Bridget never sees Lizzie until five or ten minutes after she lets Mr. Borden in the house. Additionally, Bridget stated that Lizzie entered through the front hall and that she did not know if Lizzie came from upstairs. Bridget, therefore, assumed the laugh was that of Lizzie because there was no one else other than Lizzie and Mrs. Borden at home. Bridget had no idea where either one was at that time. Lustgarten (1950) describes events surrounding Dr. Bowen's entrance to the scene.

> Doctor Bowen lived opposite. Bridget flew across the road, leaving Ms. Lizzie the sole guardian of the dead. The doctor arrived and went straight into the sitting room. He was to describe what he saw there later on the witness stand. 'Mr. Borden was lying on the lounge. His face was very badly cut, apparently with a sharp instrument; it was covered with blood.' (p. 213)

This isn't quite what was testified to at the preliminary hearing or the trial. Lizzie was not alone for very long, maybe one to one and a half minutes.

Upon the arrival of Dr. Bowen, Mrs. Churchill was also at the residence comforting Lizzie. When Bridget left the house to get Dr. Bowen, Mrs. Churchill saw her fleeing. Then Mrs. Churchill noticed Lizzie standing at the side screen door, inside the house. She called over to Lizzie and that is when Lizzie called Mrs. Churchill over to her (Brown, 1991). Also, Lustgarten suggested that Bridget went across the road to get Dr. Bowen and he returned immediately. This is how one might understand the scenario; however, that is not exactly how the events were traced. Specifically, Bridget left to find a doctor but Bowen was not home. Bridget ran back to the house and told Lizzie who then instructed her get Alice Russell. When Mrs. Churchill arrived and learned the news, she went for help and subsequently met up with John Cunningham, the news dealer. Lizzie was again left alone but not for too long. Bridget and Mrs. Churchill both saw Lizzie for a couple minutes prior to their jaunt for help and neither one saw any blood or anything else of a suspicious nature.

Two months passed between the judgment of probably guilty and the commencement of the grand jury on November 7, 1892. The grand jury heard testimony until November 15, 1892 at which time it adjourned for six days, moving in no certain direction. After Alice Russell's testimony, on December 1, 1892 the grand jury voted a true bill and a formal indictment for the murders of both Andrew and Abby Borden resulted. There were no transcripts maintained of the grand jury proceeding. There is no way to determine the precise testimony given by the witnesses; however, this was not the last step. On May 8, 1893, after a period of nine months of incarceration, Lizzie entered a formal plea of *not guilty* to the charges of the murder of Andrew and Abby Borden. A trial was set for June 6, 1893.

On Monday, June 5, 1893, a jury was picked for the trial. By the end of the selection process, twelve men had been chosen from the one hundred and eight possible jurors questioned. The District Attorney's opening statement was the downfall of the case. Just as the downfall of the investigation was the narrow path taken due to the statement that Lizzie said about Abby not being her mother, William H. Moody, counsel assisting Knowlton, set forth his opening argument which opened with a declaration that when Lizzie was questioned by police about the grizzly murders, Lizzie asserted that Abby was not her mother and that her mother was dead (Rappaport, 1992). After this statement, Moody continued with the opening remarks by plodding out the scenario as he saw it.

The defense team was led by Andrew Jennings followed by retired Governor George Robinson and Melvin Adams. The defense would have to present evidence that casts doubt on what the prosecution presents. They needed to suggest that there was another person who was the true killer and who had access to the house. They had to somehow support an alibi for Lizzie and explain some of Lizzie's actions so that a reasonable person would understand her actions and then cast doubt on the credibility of the state's witnesses. The defense does this very well with the assistance of the prosecution. In cases like this, as a jury member, one would need to depend upon critical thinking skills to sort through all of the arguments.

The trial was presided over by three judges: Justice Mason, Justice Blodgett, and Justice Dewey. The trial lasted until June 20, 1893, when Justice Dewey charged the jury for their deliberations. The following trial testimony comes from the official trial transcript. The trial presented many areas of conflicting testimony on the side of the prosecution witnesses. Regarding the murder weapon, the prosecution implied that one of the three hatchets found in the Borden residence was the murder weapon.

> The police found a hatchet whose handle had been broken off. The break was fresh. The blade was covered with coarse dust. The blade of the weapon that killed Mr. Borden was three and a half inches, exactly the size of this handleless hatchet. (Rappaport, 1992, p. 31)

Before drawing this implication, the prosecution should have determined the hatchet's value prior to the expert testimony. Dr. Edward Wood, of Harvard University, was the scientific expert who examined the hatchets. He testified that upon examination of the three hatchets, two of them that appeared to have blood stains on them tested negative for blood. Then the prosecution asked if it would be possible for the killer to use one of those hatchets, inflict the wounds as the Bordens received and then hurriedly wash the weapon so that all traces of blood would be gone in such a short time between the killings and the public discovery of the bodies. Woods answered that it would not be possible to quickly wash the hatchet and discard all traces of blood (Kent, 1992a, p. 137). Prior to this testimony, the prosecution suggested that Lizzie used this particular hatchet, quickly washed the blood off and then covered it with ash from the barn, in order to hide the evidence. Unfortunately, this was one of several downfalls for the prosecution. Had the prosecution known the answer to the question, as all lawyers should, he would have never asked the question. Several days prior to the trial commencement, Dr. Frank Draper, another scientist, graduate from Harvard and assistant to Dr. Dolan, the Medical Examiner, during the autopsies of the Bordens, sent a letter indicating to Knowlton what his testimony would be. He could basically testify to the following areas:

1. Cause and manner of death for both Andrew and Abby Borden.
2. Weapon was possibly a hatchet.
3. The length of the blade was about three and a half inches.
4. Abby Borden was killed from behind.
5. Andrew Borden was killed by blows inflicted while he lay, the killer being at the head of the sofa.
6. The killer was right handed.
7. Abby died first and Andrew died approximately one hour later.
8. Death was not instant.
9. A woman would have the ability to commit this act in the appropriate health. (Kent, 1992b, p. 136)

After listing the typical criteria for testimony, Draper added that he also found a residual of gilt metal to Abby's skull. Draper said that this metal is typical of a new hatchet never used before, an ornamental metal that hatchets are covered with after being made. The conclusion was that the hatchet had never been used. To follow that, the prosecution did not have the murder weapon because the three hatchets had all been used.

Another area of doubt created by the prosecution witnesses is the testimony regarding blood spatter. Woods testified about the amount of spatter that the killer of Andrew Borden would encounter:

Q. What part of the body would receive these spatters?

A. Above the position of the head, or from this level up. (Pointing with his hands)

Q. From the waist up?

A. Yes sir.

Q. Assuming that the assailant of Mrs. Borden stood over her when she was lying down on the floor, face downward, and taking into account the spatters of blood which you saw, have you formed an opinion as to whether her assailant would be spattered with blood?

A. I don't see how the assailant could avoid being spattered in that place.

Q. What portion of the body would receive the spatters in your opinion?

A. From the lower portion of the body and upward. (Kent, 1992b, p. 140)

This implies that the blood spatter from Abby's murder would have been to the waist and down. The same question was asked regarding the spatter to the killer of Andrew Borden and it was indicated the spatter would be obvious from the waist up. Therefore, the killer would have been covered with blood spatter and that would be difficult to hide. Every witness who saw Lizzie that morning that testified, whether for the prosecution or the defense, indicated that there was no blood observed on Lizzie's clothing or person. The Harvard issue demonstrated that the prosecution identified no murder weapon. The testimony also suggested the killer would be covered in blood, to which Lizzie was not.

As mentioned previously, regarding the letter that Dr. Draper sent the prosecution, in which he asserted the murderer was right handed, was directly contradicted by the testimony of his colleague, Dr. Dolan, the Medical Examiner. Defense counsel Adams questioned Dolan about the swing of the weapon:

Q. You think the assailant swung the instrument from left to right, don't you?

A. Yes sir.

Q. And all these wounds can be fairly accounted for by blows from left to right?

A. Yes sir.

Q. That is to say by a left-handed person?

A. Yes, by a left handed person. (Kent, 1992b, pp. 133-134)

Dolan contradicted Draper's testimony because he believed the killer was right-handed. Both experts on the same case, conducting the same tests upon the evidence resulted in conflicting conclusions. Lizzie happened to be right handed. Jennings left the issue to rest, the prosecution provided the reasonable doubt for their own witness testimony.

The police provided the same doubt when they testified as to the collection of the hatchets from the crime scene. A discrepancy occurred when Officer Michael Mullaly testified when he asked Lizzie if there were axes or hatchets in the house; Lizzie instructed Bridget to take him to the basement and show him the family tools. Mullaly stated that Bridget took him down to the basement for two hatchets and two axes which were taken from the chimney area. Then Mullaly testified that Bridget showed him a box that had a hatchet head in it. Mullaly testified that a few minutes later Officer Fleet came downstairs and Mullaly showed the weapons to him. Additionally, Mullaly said that Fleet took the hatchet from the box but also found the handle broken off within the box too. Defense counsel recalled that Fleet testified that he found the hatchet head and only the hatchet head, so it was requested the court to recall Fleet immediately. The court agreed and Fleet returned to the stand. Fleet's testimony was not quite the same as was Mullaly's:

Q. Will you state again what you found at the time you looked in (the Box)?

A. I found a hatchet head, the handle broken off, together with some other tools in there and the iron that was inside there. I don't know just what it was.

Q. You did not find the handle, the broken piece, not at all?

A. No sir.

Q. You did not see it, did you?

A. No sir.

Q. You did not see it?

A. No sir.

Q. Did Mr. Mullaly take it out of the box?

A. Not that I know of.

Q. You looked in so that you could have seen it if it was there?

A. Yes sir.

Q. You have no doubt about that, have you, at all?

A. What?

Q. That you did not find the other piece of the handle that fitted on there?

A. No sir.

Q. You saw no piece of wood with any fresh break in the box, around the box or near it?

Q. No sir, not that I am aware of. I did not see any of it. (Kent, 1992b, pp. 121-122)

The hatchet was the most valuable piece of evidence that the prosecution brought to the table in this case. Yet testimony surrounding the hatchet, the discovery and the forensic testing conducted upon all the hatchets, resulted in an overabundance of reasonable doubt created by the prosecution's own case. With contradictions in testimony of prosecution witnesses, how could any conclusions be drawn that would be deemed reliable?

Bridget Sullivan's testimony remained relatively consistent throughout each proceeding. One area of conflict was regarding whether or not she latched the screen door to the house. Bridget testified at the inquest that she did not know if she latched the screen or not. But at the trial, she testified that she did latch the screen door. During cross-examination, the defense targeted the contradiction:

Q. Are you sure you hooked the screen door? At the inquest you said that you didn't know whether you hooked it.

A. I guess I don't know whether I did or not. But it is likely that I did, because it was always kept locked.

Q. Could someone go in and out the screen door without you hearing it?

A. Yes, sir, very easily.

Q. When you were talking with Mrs. Kelly's girl, could someone have walked in the unlocked screen door without your seeing him?

A. Of course.

Q. When you were outside washing the front windows, could you see someone go in the side door?

A. Anybody could come in from the backyard, but not from the front.

Q. When you were talking with Mrs. Kelly's girl, could you see the front gate or the side gate or the sidewalk?

A. No Sir. (Rappaport, 1992, p. 56)

Bridget demonstrated that she was unsure or unclear about whether or not she latched the screen. Yet she assumed that she did, basing that assumption on the fact that she usually did. But Bridget did not have a clear recollection of whether she did or not. It was at the time of the inquest, which was closer to the time of the crime, that she testified that she really wasn't sure. After months of *questioning* with the prosecution, throughout each proceeding, Bridget became more confused. Yet, it seems more likely that she really did not know whether she had latched it or not. Take into consideration about her testimony regarding the laugh on the stairs, she assumed that the laugh came from Lizzie but did not see the person who laughed, then Bridget was not even sure if Lizzie descended the stairs prior to seeing her next.

Dr. Bowen, Mrs. Churchill, and Alice Russell were significant witnesses because they all had contact with Lizzie before the police. If anyone would have seen blood on Lizzie, it would have been one of them. Yet they all testified that they observed no blood.

Additionally, the dress that Lizzie was wearing seems to be a mystery. No one really recalled the exact dress. Lizzie described what she had on as a Bengaline silk dress. During the inquest, when she was questioned, Knowlton referred to the garment she had on the day of the murders as a skirt and a dress. He did not clarify, through Lizzie, exactly what she had on. Dr. Bowen described the dress she had on as an "ordinary, unattractive, common dress" (Rappaport, 1992, p. 61). Dr. Bowen was unable to identify if the dress the prosecution showed him was the actual dress that Lizzie wore. With all the commotion of the day, it seems that one may not take time to observe what another person is wearing, unless it was covered with blood spatter. In this case, Dr. Bowen could not recall the dress worn by Lizzie that morning.

Mrs. Churchill testified that she recalled Lizzie wore a light blue cotton dress with a navy-blue diamond figure on it. Mrs. Churchill stated that the dress the prosecution showed her did not look like the same dress as Lizzie wore that morning.

> Q. Will you describe the dress that she had on while you were there?
> A. It looked like a light blue and white groundwork. It seemed like a calico or cambric and it had a light blue and white groundwork with a dark, navy blue diamond printed on it.
> Q. Was that the dress she had on this morning? [showing her the dark blue dress Lizzie had given the police.]
> A. It does not look like it.
> Q. Was it?
> A. This is not the dress I have described. (Kent, 1992b, p. 110)

This testimony alone did not hurt the defense. But what the testimony of Alice Russell added to this was probably the most unexplained evidence during the whole trial.

> Q. Miss Russell, will you tell us what kind of a dress-give us a description of the dress that was burned, that you testified about, on Sunday morning?
> A. It was a cheap cotton Bedford cord.
> Q. What was its color?
> A. Light blue ground with a dark figure-small figure.
> Q. Do you know when she got it?
> A. I am not positive.
> Q. Well, about when she got it?
> A. In the early spring.
> Q. Was your attention called to it at the time she got it, in any way?

A. She told me she had got her Bedford cord and she had a dress-maker there and I went over there one evening and she had it on, in the very early part of the dressmaker's visit, and she called my attention to it, and I said, "Oh, you have got your Bedford cord." This is the only time I saw it until this time.

Q. Until the time it was burned?

A. Yes sir.

Q. To make it clear, between the time you saw it on Miss Lizzie Borden and had the talk about it in the spring, you did not see it again until Sunday morning after the homicide?

A. I never remember seeing it again and I am quite sure I did not-that I never did. (Kent, 1992b, p. 112)

Sounds like a wonderful prosecution witness. Prior to her testimony, she testified that she could not describe the dress that Lizzie wore the morning of the crime. Therefore, if she could be so detailed as to the dress that was burned on Sunday, but could not identify the dress that Lizzie wore the morning of the murders, the dress that was burned was likely not the dress worn the morning of the murders. The point won by the prosecution from Mrs. Churchill's testimony about the dress that was burned had actually created more doubt by this line of reasoning.

While there were other witnesses for both the prosecution and the defense, the question that emerges is whether the case should have gone as far as it did in the criminal justice system with the evidence (or lack there of) that the prosecution had. The police not only bungled the investigation but the prosecution too, through their lack of witness preparation, lack of direct evidence, and unsubstantiated circumstantial evidence. The prosecution should have been more responsible to clear those types of things up prior to any court proceeding.

There was some circumstantial evidence but it was truly clear to the prosecution that this case was more ignited through the media and public opinion rather than facts. Documents found a long time after the trial indicate that Knowlton knew there was insufficient evidence to support Lizzie's guilt but he felt almost *forced* into finding a guilty party and anybody would do.

The prosecution itself wasn't the only enemy to their case. A major blow for the prosecution was the controversial charge to the jury by Justice Dewey. Prior to his charge, Lizzie was given an opportunity to say something on her behalf. After days of listening to what a cold-hearted killer the prosecution thought she was, Lizzie simply said "I am innocent, I leave it to my counsel to speak for me" (Trial testimony). Afterwards, Justice Dewey charged the jury as to their duty to deliberate and consider all evidence and agree on a verdict. Dewey, however, presented a charge that was clearly biased and in favor of the defense. He reminded the jury of Lizzie's religious and charitable work. He tried to minimize testimony given by a witness, Mrs. Gifford, the dress maker, who stated Lizzie told her a long time before the murders not to refer to Abby as her mother because she is mean and hateful. This, Dewey stated, should not be considered as having a bearing on the murder because the statement occurred long before the murder. Dewey also told the jury that circumstantial cases can be proven beyond a reasonable doubt but failure to prove a fact essential to the case would not prove the case. He then used an example of the fact that the prosecution could not *prove* that Lizzie was in the house at the time of the murder. Dewey continued to discuss issues like the note that Abby told Lizzie she received from a sick friend. The prosecution claimed that the letter was false. Dewey suggested that it wasn't false but that the person who wrote it was not identified, the person who delivered it was not identified, and the letter had not been found. Dewey said that there was no motive presented that would lead to Lizzie making up a story about the note. Dewey reminded the jury also that there is no definite murder weapon produced from the state; therefore, they may consider that the weapon could have been any other instrument. Dewey also explained that state law provided the defendant the choice of testifying against one's self or not. He argued strongly that they should not consider the fact that she did not testify as an admission of guilt. While this may be a typical part of the jury charge, Dewey stated this, apparently, with much vigor, making a very strong impression.

This charge was not only a restatement of the defense case but it was an underlying suggestion to acquit Lizzie. At least that is what most anti-Lizzie disciples argue. At best, Justice Dewey's charge was a very liberal charge. He essentially restated the case, in support of Lizzie's defense. Additionally, the prosecution did such a good job of dismantling their own case that it is questionable as to how much influence it actually had on the jurors.

The jury deliberated approximately one hour to an hour and a half. The verdict was not guilty. Lizzie slumped into her seat and sobbed. Her ordeal was finally over. She endured losing her father, to whom she was devoted. She most likely did not have the same feeling for her stepmother. But the trauma of finding her father, being accused of killing him, being in almost every newspaper on the east coast for ten months, and having stories written about her all through various media outlets had to be taxing. At each official proceeding following the inquest, Lizzie endured many negative statements against her character. This was her time to finally release her emotions, publicly, one last time.

FURTHER FORENSIC ANALYSIS

Marcus Cicero set out for us the foundation of our criminal court system in the United States. By examining John Morse's official testimony we easily identify points of stasis that would fall under Cicero's stasis invention method. Identification of points of contention open our inquiry to significant points of interest.

Cicero is known as one of the greatest forensic orators in the Roman world. He was a phenomenal lawyer and, like many top names today, Cicero would be in high demand for his services. In his text, *de Inventione*, Cicero identified four points of stasis or the way to classify the heart of an argument where agreement diverges. These four points of contention are issues of conjecture (fact), definition, qualitative (nature of act), and translative (procedural).

Typically, when there are motions filed or objections raised in our criminal courts, the issue is usually one of these four main points. For example, conjecture disputes the facts. If there is an eyewitness testifying that a defendant was at a particular location at a particular time, a point of contention (or conjecture) would occur when the facts are disputed by offering an alibi placing the defendant in a different location at the time testified to by the witness. Stasis contentions related to definitions often refer to how something is defined. For example, what is the definition of "in custody"? Does this refer to a location or a condition of presence of an individual with a police officer? This needs to be clearly defined because the issue of advising individuals of their Miranda rights depends upon the issue of custody. If interviewing a person "in custody," whether it is in an official office, a vehicle, or at a crime scene, if that person is arrested or if I intend to arrest the person at that location, Miranda rights are necessary; otherwise, any statements will not be admissible in a court of law. However, if I question a suspect but do not intend to arrest the individual and if the individual has the right to leave when he or she wants, Miranda is not absolutely necessary. Therefore, how the idea of "custody" is defined is essential to understanding the circumstances and acting appropriately.

Next, the qualitative issue deals directly with the nature of an act. For example, there is a qualitative difference between premeditated murder, aggravated manslaughter, manslaughter, negligent homicide, and vehicular homicide. These are all acts of homicide, which means the taking of the life of one individual human being by another human being, but they are evaluated by different qualities of the act itself. Finally, a translative issue is an issue of procedure. If a person is arrested (in custody) and police gain a confession from the detainee, advisement of Miranda rights is paramount to the issue pertaining to the admissibility of the confession at a trial. If Miranda was not provided to the detainee, then the confession is not admissible per a technicality of failure to advise the Miranda rights.

We see by this brief discussion of stasis invention method that in forensic oratory there are guidelines that must be upheld. We can also see that they are not mutually exclusive and sometimes they are dependent upon each other. The definitional issue must be decided upon prior to the translative issue in this particular scenario as it depends upon the definition of "in custody" from the beginning. We can consider issues under Cicero's stasis invention method when we explore the trial testimony of John V. Morse. Let's challenge what we know and look ahead for a new under-standing of John Morse's role in the Borden murders. The next essay was originally published in *The Hatchet: Journal of Lizzie Borden Studies.*[2]

---

[2] Holba. A. (2005). The trial testimony of John V. Morse. *The Hatchet: Journal of Lizzie Borden Studies.* 2(5): 6–13.

REFERENCES

Brown, A. (1991). *Lizzie Borden: The legend, the truth, the final chapter.* New York: Dell.

Cicero, M. T. (2000). *De inventione, de optimo, genere, oratorum, topica.* Trans. H.M. Hubbell. London: Harvard University Press.

Kent, D. (1992a). *Lizzie Borden sourcebook.* Boston: Branden Publishing Company, Inc.

Kent, D. (1992b). *Forty whacks: New evidence in the life and legend of Lizzie Borden.* Emmaus, PA: Yankee Books.

Lusgarten, E. (1950). *Verdict in dispute.* New York: Scribner and Sons.

Miranda v. Arizona. 384 U.S. 436 (1966).

Rappaport, D. (1992). *Lizzie Borden trial: Be the judge, be the jury.* New York: Harper-Collins.

The Trial Testimony
of John V. Morse

If one uses a contemporary lens in an analysis of the testimony of John V. Morse in the trial of Lizzie Borden, one would conclude that the police and the prosecutor did not do a favorable, thorough, or effective job in their line of inquiry. When we critique the police, private detectives, and state personnel of the 19th century with our 21st century standards of investigation, we discover that their work was not only flawed but also inadequate. In order to give the trial testimony of John V. Morse, or any other witness in the Borden case, its due we need to stand *within* the historical moment of the given narrative episode rather than to stand above it or outside of it, however difficult that may be. Instead of accepting Morse's testimony as simply complete/incomplete or adequate/inadequate, this essay uses historicity, or authenticity, in a forensic[3] inquiry to allow us a fresh insight into Morse's contribution to the Borden case. This alternative understanding invites interested parties to reconsider John V. Morse and his enigmatic trial testimony within its own historical context. In this way, the reader may be able to more accurately evaluate John Morse's contribution to or contamination of, as the case may be, one of America's greatest unsolved mysteries.

Historicity

Historicity is a "historically effected consciousness" (Gadamer, 341) that aids us in our apprehension of a given phenomenon or circumstance. To sit outside of a historical moment and allow prejudice or a contemporary mindset to determine interpretation would be to encourage a flawed understanding of a given event. Although bias is a natural and intrinsic part of any historical interpretation, recognizing one's prejudices can help to limit their negative effects in our interpretive encounters. This does not mean, however, that we ought to ignore any foremeaning that we may come to

---

[3] "Forensic" in this case does not connote the contemporary meaning of physical evidence. Rather, the term "forensic" here is used in its rhetorical sense of the use of language and words in public oratory. Aristotle argued reserved forensic oratory as the type of speaking that attacks or defends a person. Cicero equated forensic oratory with judicial speaking that occurs in a court of law that involves accusation and defense or a claim and a counter plea of sorts.

have through our experiences. Foremeanings occupy a definite stage in our process of interpretation but their place is secondary to our historical consciousness. We should not forget our preconceptions but we should also acknowledge them while we strive to remain open to new meanings.

"Prejudice" means "a judgment that is rendered before all the elements that determine a situation have been finally examined" (Gadamer, 270). The Latin word for prejudice is *praejudicium*, which means to have an adverse effect, harm, or consequence. Having prejudgment does not guarantee a false interpretation; rather, it can have both negative and positive consequences. In this particular approach to the trial testimony of John V. Morse, I will, therefore, take care to acknowledge my own bias in the case while remaining open to finding new meaning in this rhetorical examination of his sworn responses.

The approach of this essay is through the privileging of historicity so that we do not close down potential meaning from emerging. John V. Morse is a very interesting character within the "emplotment" (Ricoeur, 31) of the Borden murders. If we limit our frame for comprehending the case or Morse's potential role in the scenario to a strictly modern mindset, we would necessarily exclude things that might enlighten our understanding of the case. We would probably also make assumptions and draw conclusions that are not based on actual conditions. Approaching our consideration of John V. Morse through historicity will aid in our quest for a clearer understanding of his role in the narrative of the life and death of Andrew and Abby Borden.

NARRATIVE

For the purpose of this essay, narrative "begins with a speech act that is tested by people and competing world views, then is fashioned into a story with main characters, a history, and a direction; a story becomes a narrative only when it is corporately agreed upon and no longer the product of an individual person" (Arnett and Arneson, 6–7). The narrative that enfolds this essay is the narrative of the life and death of Andrew Borden. Once his death became known in a public sense, Andrew Borden's life became public. The characters of emplotment within Andrew's narrative include Lizzie Borden, Emma Borden, Abby Borden, Bridget Sullivan, and John Morse, not to mention many others contained within his circle of life experience. In order for this rhetorical examination to proceed, understanding the rationality of a narrative is essential.

Humans are essentially rhetorical beings, according to Walter Fisher's (1989) narrative paradigm. Fisher considers human beings as capable of negotiating stories that often fall into the gray areas of living-in-the-world, which the rational world paradigm does not often embrace. Fisher argues that 1) human beings are story-tellers who are not always-only rational, 2) the mode of making decisions is based upon "good reasons," 3) good reasons are ruled by history, biography, culture, and character, 4) rationality is not determined by argument constructs but by narrative probability or coherence and narrative fidelity, and finally, 5) the world is a set of stories, not logical puzzles, that human beings must negotiate through, and it is through these negotiations of stories that human beings continue to create and recreate their lives.

Considering narrative as a frame for the examination of Morse's trial testimony is helpful because narrative rationality can determine flaws in the logical communicative sequence.

Narrative Coherence

Fisher considers narrative probability as that which constitutes a coherent story. This narrative coherence emerges from questions like "Can this happen this way?" and "Is it probable that these consequences will occur if this happens?" These questions are not always situated in a logical construct with experts guiding the answers. Rather, common folk, or people who live in the everyday stuff of human stories, can make decisions based upon asking these questions. Fisher attributes common sense to common people who live in the world—there is no need for an expert to tell the common folk what to believe. In the real world, there are limits to logical constructs that weaken an argument's determina-tion of rationality. Fisher believes that stories developed out of common sense experience can provide the basis for rationality just the same, and sometimes better, as rational-logical constructs.

Understanding the value of narrative coherence allows us to ask questions pertaining to the trial testimony of John V. Morse that may be different questions than those based upon a rational paradigmatic approach. This we will see as we consider whether or not Morse's responses make sense within the Borden narrative. Additionally, the approach of questioning Morse, the framing or asking of a question and the acceptance of an answer may be determined as either from a rational or a narrative framework and can help in this interpretive analysis of Morse's testimony. Along with narrative coherence, narrative fidelity is essential to a consideration of Morse's trial testimony.

NARRATIVE FIDELITY

Narrative fidelity tells us whether or not someone's story rings true and consistent with our own experiences. An example of this would be to consider someone's action or response to a particular situation and compare that reaction to our own potential reaction to a similar situation that we may have experienced. We consider what makes sense to us based upon how we live our lives. Of course narrative fidelity may be different for different people; nevertheless, part of how we evaluate what other people tell us is to compare it to what we know in our lives. By combining this aspect of interpretation with narrative coherence one can come to a reliable decision about a particular event or circumstance.

In the case of John Morse's testimony, examining narrative fidelity can point to whether or not his testimony is consistent with what we know in our lives or to what we know as truth. This is a tool that is helpful to discern those rhetorical inventions that people often use in their mode of public discourse. Narrative coherence and narrative fidelity can advance the traditional rational paradigmatic approach toward a fuller understanding of a particular communicative event.

RHETORICAL FRAMES

In order to understand something through narrative coherence we ask these questions: "Does this make sense?" "Could this happen this way?" and "Is it likely that this could have occurred?" For coherency, it is important for an answer to follow a question or for the answer to be pertinent to the question. Significant areas of Morse's testimony seem more to follow the lines of nonsequitorious response, defined as a conclusion that does not follow from the argument, question, or general relevancy, rather than a response that would be considered coherent. Nonsequitors punch holes in stories, and some of Morse's trial testimony contains these holes.

An example of John Morse's use of nonsequitor in his trial testimony occurs when the prosecutor asks him what he did when he returned from his morning errands on the day of the murders:

> Q. Where did you go then?
> A. Went to the house.
> Q. When you got to the house were you informed by any one that something had happened there?
> A. Yes, sir.
> Q. In consequence of that information did you go into the house?
> A. I did.
> Q. Which one of Mr. and Mrs. Borden did you first see?
> A. Saw Miss Lizzie.

Morse is focusing his observation on Lizzie and avoiding the explanation of his first inspection of Andrew and Abby Borden's dead bodies. Much of Morse's testimony demonstrates easy, short answers directly related to the questions. However, there are a few places within his questioning where he fails to be consistent in his answering. Another place in his testimony where his answers are not appropriate to the line of questioning pertains to biographical data:

> Q. By the way, the child of the first marriage who died [referring to Andrew Borden's biological children with his first wife], was he or she older or younger than the surviving children?
> A. She was younger than Lizzie, between the two.
> Q. Your answer is somewhat inconsistent.
> A. Well, Emma is the oldest, then Alice, her name was next, and then Lizzie.

In this case, Morse's testimony does not follow in biological sequence. These interruptions are seemingly benign answers that can potentially rupture into red herrings, which are arguments designed to take your attention away from the actual or real argument of a case. John Morse does not create red herrings but his minimal nonsequitor responses create red herrings to which the questioner has to adapt. While some of Morse's testimony was not fully developed and should have been readdressed through cross-examination or re-direct examination, issues of less importance were advanced, such as Mr. Robinson's questioning about Andrew Borden's first wife's death:

Q. Did you give correctly, do you think, the date of your sister's death – the year? I mean the first Mrs. Borden?

A. Why, I know that was just the best of my recollection, about that time. It may have been within a year or so of it, I think. I know it was during war times, and I think about the first of it too. It was during the war times.

Q. Yes. Well, now, as you recall it, do you recollect that Miss Lizzie was born in July, 1860?

A. I make it she is about 32 or 33 years old.

Q. Yes, sir. But we are not now speaking of that, but whether you did not put the date of your sister's death about a year or two too early?

A. Well, I may.

Q. Yes. Miss Lizzie was a little girl two or three years old that time, wasn't she, at the time your sister died, instead of being about a year?

A. I thought she was about three years old when he married the second time. I have got my mind that way.

Q. Well, you are not certain now, correctly, then; but upon reflection I understand you to day you cannot now positively state the year?

A. No, I cannot.

Q. You may be in error a year or two?

A. Yes.

Interestingly, this line of questioning occurs at the end of Morse's cross-examination. While it does show potential errors of Morse's reasoning, it does not aid in the clarification of other questions that are still unanswered, such as:

1. What was Morse's business in Fall River on that particular visit?
2. What were his current business dealings with Andrew Borden? (*These first two questions could have been carefully considered without violating standard hearsay rules*).
3. Why did he not bring luggage to the Borden household on this visit?
4. Why did he sleep in the guest room when in the past he slept on the third floor in a room across from Bridget Sullivan's room?
5. Why did he choose to eat pears from the yard upon his return from his business in town the day of the murders?

Morse arrived at the Borden residence, he says, at 20 minutes to 12, in time for the noon meal. If he knew he was about to have dinner, why would he munch on pears, dawdling in the back yard, before his entrance? Nevertheless, while some questions can never be answered, they should have been asked at the trial in order to make sense out of his testimony or story. These rhetorical glimpses into the forensic testimony help to unfold potential interpretive meaning. Narrative fidelity adds even more potentiality to this task.

Fidelity, Morse, and Sullivan

Truth is a difficult thing to define and determine, especially when factual evidence cannot be used as a guide. There is an important area of questioning in Morse's testimony that is inconsistent with that of Bridget Sullivan's testimony. John Morse testifies that he heard a conversation between Bridget and Abby Borden on the morning of the murders:

Q. Did you hear any conversation between Mrs. Borden and Bridget that morning?

A. Spoke to her about washing some windows.

Q. What did she say?

A. Said she would.

Q. That is Bridget said she would?

A. Yes.

Q. Give what Mrs. Borden said to Bridget?

A. I think she said in this way: "Bridget, I want you to wash these windows to-day."

Q. And about what time was that said?

A. At breakfast time.

Q. While you were seated at the table?

A. Yes, sir.

In fact, Bridget testifies that the window-washing conversation she had with Mrs. Borden occurred after John Morse left the house the morning of the murders. It is clear from the content that both Morse and Sullivan are talking about the same conversation:

Q. After you had completed your breakfast what did you do?

A. I took the dishes off out of the dining-room and brought them out in the kitchen and began to wash them.

Q. Did you complete the washing of the dishes before any one else appeared?

A. No, sir.

Q. Who next appeared?

A. The next I remember to see was Mr. Borden and Mr. Morse going out the back entry – the back door.

Q. Did Mr. Morse return after the two went out to the screen door?

A. No, sir; he went out.

Q. Did Mr. Borden return at that time?

A. Yes, sir.

Q. You will have to speak a little louder?

A. Mrs. Borden was in the dining-room as I was fixing my dining-room table, and she asked me if I had anything to do this morning. I said, No, not particular, if she had anything to do for me. She said she wanted the windows washed. I asked her how, and she said inside and outside both, they are awful dirty.

Q. What was she doing when you had that talk with her in the dining-room?

A. She was dusting. She had a feather duster in her hand. She was dusting between the sitting-room and dining-room, the door.

Apparently, according to Bridget Sullivan's testimony, it was shortly after she cleaned the breakfast dishes that John Morse left for the morning, an event that occurred before the Abby conversation. John Morse testified that he heard the conversation, and he related the specifics, but he claimed it occurred during breakfast. It seems as though Morse did hear this conversation because he relates similar content of the conversation as Bridget. From the perspective of narrative fidelity, the conflicting claims of this argument suggest that there is a question of truth to these statements. We know that someone is not being truthful because the answer cannot be both ways.

The only two people who can confirm or deny the truthfulness of either of these statements were killed. We may not be able to determine which statement is absolutely truthful to the facts but we can safely state that someone is not being truthful. Therefore, narrative fidelity cannot be achieved through these two people's stories. While we can look at the overarching coherency of Bridget Sullivan's testimony and compare it to the overarching coherency of Morse's testimony and determine who is likely to be telling the truth, without corroboration of the facts, narrative fidelity can never be truly attained, thus making it difficult to come to an accurate understanding of the situation. How do we, then, successfully interpret within the given historical moment of the trial of Lizzie Borden? We have to consider the implications of Morse's testimony and continue to compare it to Bridget Sullivan's testimony, point by point, so that we can at least determine, through good reasons, which witness is more likely to be accurate overall.

FIDELITY, MORSE, AND THE TESTIMONY
OF OTHERS

There is another important area in the questioning of Morse that is inconsistent with the testimony of others. John Morse testifies that he left his relatives on Weybosset Street at 20 minutes past 11 and immediately took a horse car to the corner of Pleasant and Second Street, then walked directly to the Borden house, arriving at 20 minutes to 12. He is asked about his arrival:

> Q. When you got to the Borden house did anything attract your attention at first?
> A. No, sir.
> Q. Where did you first go?
> A. Went into the back door, round the rear part of the house, to a pear tree.
> Q. Did you do anything out there?
> A. Picked up two or three pears.
> Q. Did you begin to eat them or not?
> A. I ate part of one of them.
> Q. Where did you go then?
> A. Went to the house.

Police Officer George Allen, however, testifies that he arrived at the murder scene for the second time at half past 11, but no later than 25 minutes to 12, and saw several people gathered outside in the road. That Morse could walk past the side door that was being guarded by Charles Sawyer, eat a pear in the back yard (before dinner) and not see or hear anyone or anything unusual confounds us.

There is yet another area of conflicting testimony, this time during the preliminary hearing. Patrick Doherty, upon first visiting the guest room where Mrs. Borden's body lay, had moved the bed "away from her head" to make the space wider. He then went to telephone the station, and when he returned spoke to Bridget a few minutes in the kitchen. He then went upstairs, returning to the guest room, and implies Dr. Dolan was also in the room. In his preliminary hearing testimony Doherty states:

> I saw Mr. Morse in the room when I got back from the telephone, when I was looking at Mrs. Borden's body. He stood in the room with his hand on the foot of the bed.

Morse, on the other hand, testifies thusly at the preliminary:

Q. You went up the front stairs, did you go up into the room?
A. No sir.
Q. How far did you go?
A. Probably two-thirds of the way up, so I could look under the bed.
Q. What do you mean by "look under the bed"?
A. When I got up high enough, I could look through the space under the bed, and saw Mrs. Borden laying there between the bed and the bureau.
Q. Did you know she was up in that room?
A. They told me so.

One could assume, based on narrative fidelity, that Morse would have remembered the experience of closely observing the gruesome remains of his brother-in-law's wife and that this would be something he would retain in his mind's eye and could recall later. Oddly, Morse chooses not to place himself near her body for some inexplicable and unknowable reason.

Implications of Morse's Testimony

The trial testimony transcripts of the Lizzie Borden case can easily be obtained and read by any person who downloads them from Lizzie-AndrewBorden.com. The difficult part follows in the interpretation of witness testimony. We have to be careful not to prejudge the testimonies by our contemporary standards of judgment. Through Court TV and other forms of media, the legal process of criminal trials has become familiar to most people in the Western World. Without withholding my contemporary prejudices, I might be inclined to reduce my interpretation of this case to flawed police inquiries, a flawed criminal investigation, poor use of forensic science, and other setbacks that the television series *Cold Case Files* might choose to investigate.

When we argue a point in the past from the position in the present we may fall prey to prejudices that will close down the inquiry. Looking at Morse's testimony through universal frames of inquiry, such as classical rhetorical theory and contemporary communication theory, we work within the guidelines of historicity, which can keep the horizon of our inquiry in sight, inviting new ways of seeing old things.

CONCLUSION

Leonard Rebello's *Lizzie Borden Past and Present* is a comprehensive, well-documented reference for the Borden murders and the period in which they occurred. The purpose for a comprehensive text of this magnitude is to provide a hermeneutic entrance into the nuances involved in a case of such social, political, and cultural magnitude. We hope that by closely studying the case of the Borden murders we can learn something about the past and apply it to our understanding of the present. While there are many methods for studying historical events, there are also flaws to our process. Therefore, considering alternative methods in interpreting experiences can shed some much needed new light on preexisting circumstances.

This essay has examined episodes in the trial testimony of John V. Morse allowing historicity to be our interpretive beacon to help us to see communicative exchanges in alternative ways. It can be used as a guide for further reflection upon our potential acceptance of narratives involved in the Borden inquiry. This approach reminds us to be cautious in our examinations of historical texts, while being aware that logic or rational approaches to interpretation can sometimes be limiting. Narrative rationality can offer our interpretive encounters a richer outcome. Future scholarship in Borden studies might consider using historicity and narrative to reconsider other aspects of this most interesting and perplexing case.

References

Arnett, R.C., & Arneson, P. (1999). *Dialogic civility in a cynical age: Community, hope, and interpersonal relationships.* New York: SUNY Press.

Cicero, M. T. (2000). *De inventione, de optimo, genere, oratorum, topica.* Suffolk, UK: St. Edmundsbury Press, Ltd.

Fisher, W. R. (1989). *Human communication as narration: Toward a philosophy of reason, value, and action.* Columbia, SC: University of South Carolina Press.

Gadamer, H.G. (2002). *Truth and method.* New York: Continuum.

Rebello, L. (1999). *Lizzie Borden past & present: A comprehensive reference to the life and times of Lizzie Borden.* Fall River, MA: Al-Zach Press.

Ricoeur, P. (1984). *Time and narrative.* vol. 3. Chicago: University of Chicago Press.

QUESTIONS FOR DISCUSSION
ON CHAPTER 5

1. Identify the categories of Cicero's stasis invention method.
2. Provide an example of a translative issue in this case.
3. Define narrative coherence.
4. Define narrative fidelity.
5. Can you think of other contemporary cases where the issue of historicity has come into the discussion?
6. What other recent public/political situations involve issues of narrative?
7. Identify the points of stasis in this case. Take a current events issue and explore similar points of contention. How different or similar are these scenarios today?

CHAPTER 6

THE LIZZIE BORDEN
NARRATIVE

Walter Fisher's narrative paradigm was introduced in the preceding chapter. Remember that narrative framework as we now take a look at the narrative in which Lizzie Borden lived. Her story is not so much different from many stories today. We can find a more textured under-standing now by expanding our own understanding of Lizzie Borden's story by adding to our inquiry the idea of the performance paradigm as posited by Kathleen Glenister Roberts, in her essay entitled, "Texturing the Narrative Paradigm: Folklore and Communication,"[1] where she offers texture to Fisher's narrative paradigm through performance and culture. This offers ethnographic extension to the narrative framework.

A narrative is born when a story is accepted by a large number of people (Arnett & Arneson, 1999). A narrative "begins with a speech act that is tested by people and competing world views, then is fashioned into a story with main characters, a history, and a direction; a story becomes a narrative only when it is corporately agreed upon and no longer the product of an individual person" (Arnett & Arneson, 1999, p. 7). Kathleen Roberts extends this definition to include "a genre of communication, even a basis for ethical decision-making" (2004, p. 129). Considering narrative experiences from an ethnographic framework provides texture to our

---

[1] It is recommended that this essay be read in conjunction with this chapter. Roberts, K. G. (2004). Texturing the narrative paradigm: Folklore and communication. *Communication Quarterly. 52*(2), 129–142.

understanding of how narratives work in a communication framework. According to Roberts (2004), performance happens when "individuals *act* in artful performances that have meaning and texture for their social group. They do not simply react to the pressures of a culture that exists outside their agency" (p. 135). The artful performance does not need to be professional or masterful. The performance simply must evoke emotion that has potential to call forth others into the narrative. Sometimes the performances are surprises and sometimes they transform experiences and tradition into something new. These performances are utterances, stories, and symbolic actions that unite people through emotion. The performance paradigm provides a way for human agents to evaluate narrative coherence and narrative fidelity. Performances do not exist outside the individual performances rather these performances resonate between performers and serve to bring people together. Through these artful performances we test coherence and fidelity of the narrative in which we are situated.

The performances in which Lizzie was part include her call for help after she found her father dead, her interview/interrogation by the police, her inquest testimony, her behavior in jail while awaiting trial, and her choreographed performance each day of the trial. Additionally, her act of burning the dress while under house arrest in the days following the murders and her early and innocent statement to the police investigator when she indicated that Abby Borden was not her mother—that her mother had died when she was a young child—are also performances that enabled the police and the public to test her narrative coherence and fidelity. The burning of her dress was explicitly a ritualized performance that called attention to her actions, her potential motive, and her potential self-incrimination that called forth the authorities into action. In this case, the action was the formal indictment on the criminal charges of murder. Did her performances make sequential sense and did they ring true with what is typically known to be true?

It is essential to recognize how we use coherence and fidelity in our communicative exchanges and decision-making. As well, it is important to be able to evaluate coherence and fidelity if we are using them as a basis for our own thoughts and actions. The following essay was published in *The Hatchet: Journal of Lizzie Borden Studies*[2] and implicitly teaches

---

[2] Holba, A. (2004). The rhetoric of gender bias in Victorian New England: The ongoing dialectic. *The Hatchet: Journal of Lizzie Borden Studies. 1*(1), 44–49.

us much about the narrative of Lizzie Borden. Consider the historical narrative in which Lizzie lived. Consider Lizzie's role in gender narratives during the suffragist movement. Consider how ignorance permeated the narrative structures in which Lizzie's experiences unfolded. All of these considerations open our understanding and comprehension as we try to make sense of this mystery.

References

Arnett, R.C., & Arneson, P. (1999). *Dialogic civility in a cynical age: Community, hope, and interpersonal relationships.* New York: SUNY Press.

Roberts, K. G. (2004). Texturing the narrative paradigm: Folklore and communication. *Communication Quarterly. 52*(2), 129–142.

THE RHETORIC OF GENDER BIAS
IN VICTORIAN NEW ENGLAND:
THE ONGOING DIALECTIC

The Lizzie Borden case of 1892 is often compared to the O.J. Simpson case of 1994 because both involved seemingly guilty defendants who were acquitted of the murder of two people due to insufficient evidence *and* popular notions of bias, racial or gender played a significant role in their verdicts. In both cases the police were also accused of bumbling their investigations, which led to issues pertaining to the *fruit of the poisonous tree* evidentiary exclusions and charges that the police failed in their duty to gather enough evidence to convict. Central to the Lizzie–O.J. line of reasoning is the belief that they both actually committed the crimes and, consequently, a gross miscarriage of justice occurred with their acquittals. Yet, the major argument linking these two cases would fall like a house of cards if either Lizzie or O.J. were truly innocent. Without dispute, however, is the second comparison, namely, that both criminal justice systems, at the times of the murders, reacted out of bias based on fear and ignorance and, it can be argued, that this same bias was responsible for both Lizzie and O.J. enjoying quick acquittals. The purpose for this inquiry, then, is to enter the discourse about the impact of gender bias as it specifically relates to the Borden murder case and examine how this bias fueled ignorance rather than justice.

Working from the assumption that we all have been exposed to the Borden narrative, I ground my claims in the official testimony taken from the inquest, preliminary hearing, and trial, newspaper reports of the grand jury proceedings, and the recently published correspondence of Borden case prosecutor Hosea Knowlton. In considering the relationship between gender bias and the events encountered, it is revealed that the rhetoric of gender bias significantly influenced the disposition of the investigation and the complete legal case. Through a close examination of dialectic encounters between Lizzie, the accused, and several officials involved in the legal matter, it becomes clear that gender bias and gender fear was prevalent in the rhetoric that directed human communication. True to the historical moment, laden within the social and legal tapestry, the rhetoric of gender bias was clear and present in 1892, Victorian New England.

At the time the Borden murders occurred, criminal investigation in America was maturing from a force of unskilled watchmen to a professional community of multidisciplinary experts. While at the beginning stages of this professionalization phase in law enforcement, media interest in crime was also flourishing. Combined, police and reporters would allow the public to actually *see* the crime and follow every aspect of the case. The Borden case would change the face of how America would see crime and criminal investigations forever. While this alone is a topic for future discussion, it also is the avenue for how the rhetoric of gender bias could have influenced so many involved in the case.

GENDER BIAS

Gender bias is difficult to define and measure. A dictionary definition says that for a bias to exist there must be one to whom it belongs (*Oxford English Dictionary*, p. 223). It is a point of view. Bias means to have a slanted or unreasoned temperament towards something or someone. It could be deliberate or involuntary. In order to have this temperament one must possess a particular judgment about something or someone. In the case of gender bias, this would include a predetermined judgment about someone, something, or a certain action or statement. This judgment may cause a certain response, which would therefore prejudice any outcome. Joanne Belknap (2001) says that "discrimination against women is more often motivated by paternalism" (p. 330). Julia Wood (2006), in her book, *Gendered lives: Communication, gender and culture*, suggests that there is still inequity against women based upon bias in today's society.

In the case of Lizzie Borden, the accused axe murderer of her biological father and stepmother, the criminal justice system reacted through the gender bias of Victorian New England. Society, one hundred years ago, was structured much differently than today. In order to analyze what happened in Fall River on August 4, 1892, one must consider the attitudes of the time. The social and familial hierarchy in Victorian New England included the family as a nurturing and peaceful refuge away from the harsh reality of the soon to be industrial revolutionized world. Women were the managers of their households and subjugated to their husbands or fathers. Men worked interchangeably between their private and public spheres. The ideal situation would include marriage, children, servants, a respectable house, and the opportunity to interact in the community. It would be appropriate for the unmarried women to engage suitors, volunteer in charitable organizations, or service at their local church. According to Mary Shanley (1989), historian in gender studies, "Women presided over the home, while men sallied forth into the public realm" (p. 3). Additionally, she says, "the family was a locus of male power sustained by the judicial authority of the state" (p. 4). As far as the duties women were expected to engage, Shanley states, "In addition to bearing children, middle class women directed and working class women performed, the work involved in maintaining the household—care of the children, sewing, cooking, and cleaning" (p. 5). Generally, women had a place in society that was socially constructed by a male-dominated culture.

Lizzie, the unmarried woman, did not work outside the home. Her father was a respectable businessman and had several thriving ventures to occupy his time. Lizzie did not need to work for financial reasons but spent her time teaching Sunday school and participating in volunteer activities with the local chapter of a Women's Christian Temperance League. Nothing is factually known about her romantic interests. There have been innuendoes about a few possible suitors; however, there is nothing to suggest that Lizzie was involved in any serious relationship. Lizzie was thirty-two years old, unmarried, and living at home with her father, stepmother, older sister, and the family servant.

Typical patriarchal attitudes of the time would consider Lizzie less likely to be marriageable but still under her father's domain. Even though Abby Borden married Andrew when Lizzie was about five years of age, after her biological mother died unexpectedly, Lizzie did not entertain the notion that Abby should be respected as her *mother*. Emma, Lizzie's older sister by seven years, apparently assumed the role as caretaker of Lizzie when their mother died. It was rumored that Andrew married Abby out of convenience—to secure someone to run his household and to provide child-care for his two daughters. In fact, it has been speculated that both Lizzie and Emma considered Abby a mere servant (Kent, 1992a).

In our historical moment there is no reason to believe this to be a suspicious statement, "She is not my mother, sir. She is my stepmother. My mother died when I was a child." This was Lizzie's answer to a question asked by an official in Fall River, after the discovery of Andrew Borden's body, during the initial phase of the investigation. Her response was simple and clear. Abby Borden was not her mother. Abby Borden was her stepmother and her biological mother was no longer living. Lizzie merely clarified her relationship with Abby Borden. Common in our postmodern era, there is a much higher divorce rate and a more liberal attitude toward the family unit, as society today seems to be rethinking and reshaping the idea of what a family might look like. Lizzie's comment today would certainly be recorded but it would not be allowed to shape the investigation. However, in August of 1892, that statement, coming from a woman, was simply against all norms of society. In the eyes of the male authorities, Lizzie had erred against the institution of family and the authority of her patriarchal society. The next wrong assumption would then conclude that she hated Abby, enough to kill her.

During the trial of Lizzie Borden, police officials testified that Lizzie's statement defining her relationship with Abby was their first clear indication that she should be the main suspect. Of course, no respectable girl would consider devaluing the worth of a family unit like Lizzie did, unless, of course, she was the murderer. This was the hyper-masculine reaction to a perceived threat to the nucleus of the American Family, which was the foundation of their patriarchal society. Once this statement was made, there was very little investigation into the death of Andrew and Abby Borden unless it dealt with pooling evidence against Lizzie, for the criminal investigators knew their *murderess* and would stop at nothing to prove it.

GENDER FEAR

The criminal justice system of 1892, then, reacted out of *gender fear*. Lizzie's statement to them was perceived as a threat that intended to undermine their authority in society. Coinciding with the gender bias claim, these male authoritative figures knew the women's movement was forming and active. Patriarchal society was struggling against this backdrop to maintain its structure. How could they allow a spinster woman to decide for herself that a stepmother might not be a valid member of the familial structure? Andrew, the head of his household, had decided to remarry and bring Abby into their lives. It was not Lizzie's place to question that decision, for to allow that questioning would diminish the power that a man had over a woman and that a father had over his daughter. Township officials and police involved in the investigation became more concerned with society and what it was thinking than solving the crime.

As this gender bias and gender fear manipulated the investigation, it resulted in the loss of evidence unrelated to Lizzie, as anything else was either deemed insignificant or could be explained away. Due to their fear of losing the patriarchal authority that they were used to, they had to try and convict her at all cost. In this passionate derailment they lost the true sight of what they should have been following—they forgot about solving the crime. The prosecutor and Attorney General knew they had no evidence that could logically be linked to Lizzie and that if they pursued the case in a criminal forum they would lose. This is documented in a memo sent to Attorney General Pillsbury from the prosecutor Knowlton, in which he details the obligation to pursue the matter in formal court proceeding only because of the media hype and to maintain appearance of doing something:

> I note your suggestions about form of indictment which I will adopt if we ever get so far: of which, however, I am far from certain. (Kent, 1992a)

A second memo:

> Personally I would like very much to get rid of the trial of the case, and fear that my own feelings in that direction may have influenced my better judgment […] I confess, however, I cannot see my way clear to any disposition […] even though there is reasonable expectation of a verdict of not guilty. (Kent, 1992a, Centerfold)

Once the investigation became slanted and focused only on Lizzie, the evidence that was obtained had to be manipulated in order to link it to Lizzie. For example, the hatchet found in the basement of her house was assumed to be the murder weapon. The media presented many articles about the hatchets that were discovered in the house and how they could be linked to Lizzie. Yet the hatchet was quite a common instrument to be found at anyone's house, especially at the turn of the century, when chopping the heads off of chickens and cutting firewood might be a daily activity. It would not have been unusual to find several hatchets at most of the homes on the same street where she lived. Further, upon scientific examination of these hatchets, no human blood was ever identified. It was determined by scientists at Harvard University that the blood on the hatchet was, in fact, animal blood. While courtroom testimony indicated that one hatchet was the size of the instrument that impacted the victims, so were hundreds of other hatchets.

Another example of the manipulation of evidence involved a dress that Lizzie burned while under guard by the Fall River police. After the police conducted three separate searches of the house and during a period following the crimes when the police were positioned outside the house to guard it and observe the comings and goings of its inhabitants, no evidence implicating Lizzie was found nor was there any police report of any evidence being removed from the house. During the course of her confinement and as Emma cleaned the house (crime scene), Lizzie burned a dress that had been soiled by paint three months prior to the murders. The dress was burned in their stove and Lizzie's good friend, Alice Russell, witnessed her tearing it up at the stove. During the grand jury phase of the investigation, after an extended period of adjournment, Russell came forward and testified that Lizzie burned a soiled dress. According to the transcripts of the inquest and the preliminary hearing, Alice Russell had said nothing about the dress-burning incident. It was only when Ms. Russell asked for and was granted the chance to amend her previous testimony that the tale was officially told. Alice's grand jury revelation proved to be the deciding factor to indict Lizzie and hold her for trial. At this point it was too late for officials to examine the dress for what might or might not be present. As overkill would prevail, Lizzie was formally charged with three counts of murder, one for Andrew Borden, one for Abby Borden, and another count for both of the victims.

Instead of asking additional investigative questions prior to the indictment, the prosecution subsequently lost the persuasiveness of their evidence when the truth came out about the dress and the burning. Through an independent witness it was supported that there was paint on the dress prior to the murders and that Emma instructed Lizzie to burn it when she did. One question to consider is where was the dress during all three of the house searches prior to the burning? Either the police overlooked it or its value as evidence was not as inflammatory as officials later suggested.

RHETORICAL OVERREACH

As their ignorance led them to lose what little circumstantial evidence they had, police overlooked significant areas of examination. They accepted the testimony of the maid, Bridget Sullivan, too quickly, as well as the alibi of John Morse, Andrew's brother-in-law. The strongest point that suggests a need for further inquiry may have moved the investigation in a different direction. Bridget testified that the morning of the murders she was not feeling well. However, Abby Borden instructed her to wash the windows, inside and out. Bridget testified that these instructions were given to her *after* John Morse left for a business/social engagement that morning. In Morse's original inquest testimony, he offers that he heard Abby Borden give these instructions to Bridget. In a timeline constructed through documented testimony, Bridget claims she received these instructions at least ten minutes after Morse left the residence. This conflict constitutes a major discrepancy and needed further inquiry. If Bridget's testimony is accurate and the most consistent, and if Morse did hear the instructions given to Bridget by Abby, he would have been in the house after he officially left. However, police did not pursue further inquiry in this direction. Both situations cannot be true. After analysis of Bridget's testimony, which was very lengthy and detailed, throughout the inquest, preliminary hearing, grand jury, and trial, she remained consistent in all aspects. John Morse simply was not asked.

In addition to this inadequate inquiry, the prosecutor violated Lizzie's right to be represented by counsel at the inquest by failing to advise her of that right. At the time of the murders, Massachusetts law allowed for legal representation if one was the subject of a criminal investigation. Lizzie was forced to testify at an inquest for three days, without counsel, as the judge and prosecutor both believed that each other had formally advised Lizzie of the right to counsel. How could both professional men *assume* the other had given the advisement? Is it realistic, then, for us to believe that no deception was intended? I believe that both the prosecutor and judge intended to deceive Lizzie in order to get her *confession*. After all, she was merely a woman who stood to undermine their patriarchal privilege of power and control.

During her inquest testimony, Lizzie was under the influence of morphine, as prescribed by Dr. Bowen, the Borden family physician. Dr. Bowen testified at the trial that Lizzie was under the influence of double the normal dosage of morphine. Authors and scholars have used the fact of Lizzie's medicated state to support their assertions that her testimony at the inquest was compromised and her thoughts jumbled as she gave conflicting statements as to her whereabouts the morning of the murders. While some of her testimony may have been unclear, after an objective review of Lizzie's inquest testimony, and with eleven years experience as a prosecutor's detective in a Major Crimes Unit, I suggest that the questions presented by the prosecutor were leading, deceptive, and manipulative, and that Lizzie was not the victim of a morphine induced state of confusion, but, rather, that she was provoked by an expert prosecutor to *appear* to indict herself in the crimes by *seeming* contradictions of fact.

For example, a deceitfully leading line of questioning that the prosecutor pursued involved his persistent questioning regarding her whereabouts when her father returned home the day of the murders, the frequency of John Morse's visits, and Lizzie's search for lead in a box in the barn. The implication of his pursuit is that her answers weren't "right" and he needed to direct her to answer them again until he found the answer that he wanted. Deception is part of police investigations but in the court room there is a fine line between trickery and deception. First, as I mentioned earlier, the circumstances surrounding Lizzie's inquest testimony was deceptive. Also, in the questioning regarding Lizzie's whereabouts at the time of her father's return, the prosecutor blatantly uses tactics to confuse her. On day two of the inquest, the following occurs:

> Q. (Knowlton, Prosecutor) Now I call your attention to the fact that yesterday you told me, with some explicitness, that when your father came in, you were just coming down stairs.
> A. No, I did not. I beg your pardon.
> Q. That you were on the stairs at the time your father was let in, you said with some explicitness. Do you now say you did not say so? (Kent, 1992b)

The result of this line of questioning was that Lizzie appeared to be changing her story and the prosecutor looked like he "caught her." But after review of her testimony on day one, the prosecutor actually changed her words. Specifically, Lizzie initially stated that she was in the kitchen when her father came home. However, after the prosecutor asked this same question several times (implying her answer was not "correct") he managed to gain several different answers from a morphine-influenced Lizzie as to her whereabouts. After Lizzie became totally confused on day one of the inquest regarding this issue, Lizzie would later clear up her position.

> I don't know what I have said. I have answered so many questions and I am so confused I don't know one thing from another. I am telling you just as nearly as I know how (Kent, 1992b).

After this frustrated outburst by Lizzie, she asserts at least twice that she was in the kitchen when her father came home the day of the murders, which was her original answer to the question. The prosecutor should have reviewed his notes of her testimony for day one. By asking her numerous times as to her whereabouts, he was attempting to mislead her and distort her ability to answer. His questions on day two were based upon her answers from questions on day one. This was his deceptive effort to gain that "confession."

Lastly, the prosecutor was also manipulative in his direct questioning. For example, on day one of the inquest, Lizzie stated that she did go upstairs, at one point, to sew a piece of tape on a garment. On day two the prosecutor refers to this circumstance:

> Q. You mean you went upstairs to sew a button on?
> A. I basted a piece of tape on.
> Q. Do you remember that you did not say that yesterday?
> A. I don't think you asked me. I told you yesterday I went upstairs directly after I came up from down cellar, with the clean clothes. (Kent, 1992a)

Lizzie is truthful here. She did not tell him she went to sew a button, but the prosecutor wanted her to agree with him, in order to demonstrate that she presents inconsistent testimony. The prosecutor is wrong—Lizzie never mentioned she went to sew on a button. This leads us to believe the prosecution was either ill prepared or calculatingly deceptive in his attempt to make Lizzie look like a liar.

In her testimony, Lizzie remained as consistent as she could, considering the impact of the morphine. As a matter of fact, I consider that the prosecutor at times became frustrated with his inability to trip her up or confuse her. During the prosecutor's questions regarding the fishing lines at the farm and the reasons why Lizzie would have to look for sinkers before going fishing, he seemed to get frustrated because he could not "control" Lizzie's answers.

> Q. What was the use of you telling me a while ago you had no sinkers on your line at the farm?
> A. I thought I made you understand that those lines at the farm were no good to use.
> Q. Did you not mean for me to understand one of the reasons you were searching for sinkers was that the lines you had at the farm, as you remembered then, had no sinkers on them?
> A. I said the lines at the farm had no sinkers.
> Q. I did not ask you what you said. Did you not mean for me to understand that? (Kent, 1992a)

The questioning here demonstrates that Lizzie was going to answer questions without being manipulated by the prosecutor, and he seemed frustrated that he couldn't get her to answer how he wanted her to answer.

DISPOSITION

Gender bias most definitely guided and manipulated this investigation and the disposition impacting Lizzie Andrew Borden during one of the most difficult periods in her life. Interestingly, it is this same gender bias that proved to save her life and find her innocent of the horrific crimes. In addition to the fact that there was not one piece of evidence that linked Lizzie directly to the murders, Lizzie was acquitted because the all-male jury based their verdict on this awful question—could *my* daughter, wife, or sister kill *me*? At this time in Victorian New England, the answer to this question would have to be *no*. For if their answer would be any other it would set the stage for the decline of patriarchy in their community. In 1892 Fall River, violent crime involving women did occur, but with the female as the victim, not generally as the perpetrator. Without a tradition of woman-on-man crime, the male populace of the case (i.e. the judges, jury, police, and newspapermen) was content to accuse, but not convict, a woman of the outrageously brutal and sadistic acts of patricide and matricide. Lizzie's punishment for her crimes, then, was the ordeal of her trial, and her ostracization by Fall River was her life sentence.

My intention for this essay was to not only show the complicated nature of the case but to suggest that to define Lizzie as either being guilty or innocent is a flawed contention based upon fallacies of logic grounded in gender bias. To make the assumption of her innocence or guilt, either alone or with an accomplice, one must hold tight to far too many disconnected assumptions, rendering understanding and clarity out of reach. It is my hope, especially with this new journal, *The Hatchet: Journal of Lizzie Borden Studies,* that the narrative of Lizzie Borden will live on and we will continue to be engaged in a dialectic that is finally outside the rhetoric of gender bias.

References and Bibliography

Belknap, J. (2001). *The invisible woman: Gender, crime, and justice.* Belmont, CA: Wadsworth.

Flynn, R. (1985). Foreword. In Edwin Porter, *The Fall River tragedy: A history of the Borden murders.* Portland, ME: King Phillip Publishing Co.

Gustafson, A. (1985). *Guilty or innocent?* New York: Holt, Rinehart and Winston.

Hunter, Evan. (1984). *Lizzie.* New York: Arbor House.

Kent, D. (1992a). *The Lizzie Borden sourcebook.* Boston: Branden Publishing Company, Inc.

Kent, D. (1992b). *Forty whacks: New evidence in the life and legend of Lizzie Borden.* Emmaus, PA: Yankee Books.

Kronenwetter, M. (1986). *Free press v. fair trial.* New York: Franklin Watts.

Lincoln, V. (1967). *A private disgrace: Lizzie Borden by daylight.* New York: G.P. Putnam's and Sons.

Lustgarten, E. (1950). *Verdict in dispute.* New York: Charles Scribner and Sons.

Muraskin, R. (2001). *It's a crime: Women and justice.* Upper Saddle River, NJ: Prentice Hall.

Radin, E. (1961). *Lizzie Borden: The untold story.* New York: Simon & Schuster.

Rappaport, D. (1992). *Be the judge, be the jury: The Lizzie Borden trial.* New York: Harper Collins.

Rebello, L. (1999). *Lizzie Borden past & present: A comprehensive reference to the life and times of Lizzie Borden.* Fall River, MA: Al-Zach Press.

Shanley, M. L. (1989). *Feminism, marriage, and the law in Victorian New England.* Princeton, NJ: Princeton University Press.

Showalter, E. (1997). *Hystories.* New York: Columbia University Press.

Spiering, F. (1984). *Lizzie.* New York: Random House.

Sullivan, R. (1974). *Goodbye Lizzie Borden.* Brattleboro, VT: Stephen Greene Press.

Wood, J. (2006). *Gendered lives: Communication, gender, culture.* Belmont, CA: Wadsworth.

PUBLIC INFORMATION ACKNOWLEDGMENT

Inquest Testimony of Lizzie Borden

QUESTIONS FOR DISCUSSION
ON CHAPTER 6

1. Define narrative paradigm in your own words.
2. How does Arnett and Arneson define narrative?
3. How does Roberts define narrative?
4. How does the performance paradigm texture Fisher's narrative paradigm?
5. Can you think of other contemporary cases where the issue of narrative has come into the discussion?
6. What other recent public/political situations teach us about narrative?
7. In current events, in what ways does narrative matter?

CHAPTER 7

AFTER ALL THESE YEARS

After considering numerous aspects from this case of the Borden murders as we have in this rhetorical inquiry, there is one important question that emerges: why is there still so much interest in this case in general? One answer might be that every century has its hallmarks. Specific to the United States, a few examples might include: 1) the twentieth century's turmoil of the 1960s that erupted in political assassination and advancements in race and gender rights, 2) the nineteenth century's industrial revolution, and 3) the eighteenth century's American Revolution. In the case of Lizzie Borden's story, it was a case that involved parricide, a particular form of murder that seems most foul. The accused, being a woman, held significant importance because of the suffrage movement; a woman's right to vote propelled a very public discussion on the rights of women. Of course, Lizzie's indictment by a patriarchal system would become paramount to the movement itself. The criminal case holds historical significance to the field of criminology because this is one of the early murder cases in the history of the United States where crime scene photography was utilized. Hence, the photographs of Andrew and Abby Borden are historical artifacts that tell not only a story of murder but become part of the pictorial narrative of forensic science.

Another point that heralds significance to this case is the ditty itself because it is memorable and child-like in nature, but like the original Grimm Brothers' tales, it tells a gruesome story of murder that borders the unbelievable for that historical moment. Added to this is the notion of mystery, because Lizzie never admitted to the crime, she was acquitted of the crime, but the crime was never reinvestigated. Therefore, the investigation is anticlimactic in the sense that there is no resolution, so we keep waiting for the end to near and it never does.

Finally, another possibility for the scholarly and popular venue of continued interest in Lizzie Borden has to do with the responsiveness of potentialities to changing historical moments. In the 1980s child sexual abuse cases were prevalent in the media. News reports propagated stories of sexual abuse of children, day care centers were being targeted with allegations of child sex abuse, the Catholic Church was confronted with explosive amounts of sex abuse allegations perpetrated by priests, and the film industry began to replicate these stories in the cinema and on television, bringing this dark narrative of child sexual abuse into every household. It was no surprise when theories of sexual abuse of Lizzie Borden, by her father, began to emerge, and they did. Of course many other theories continue to emerge; however, the Lizzie narrative lent itself to be responsive to the historical moment by being open to the possibility of sexual abuse. In line with the idea that the Lizzie narrative is open to possibilities and therefore holds our curiosity open and attentive to it, the next essay considers Lizzie's sexual orientation theories that hold significant import today. This essay was previously published in *The Hatchet: Journal of Lizzie Borden Studies, 4*(2), 6–13.

LIZZIE AS "DEVIANT" OTHER: INTERPRETATION OF OTHERNESS

It has been well over 100 years since Lizzie Andrew Borden was charged, tried, and acquitted for the murders of her father and stepmother. Yet, since then, no other investigation, arrest, or conviction prevailed in that legal action. In fact, the mystery that permeates this case is more dynamic than ever. One area in which the Borden murders has been explored (and exploited) is the hypothetical investigation into the sexual orientation of the only person accused of the crimes. Authors who interpret her as a guilty murderer have raised questions as to Lizzie Borden's lesbian tendencies. Why is it that Lizzie must be identified as a "deviant" other in order to explain her culpability?

There were hundreds of newspaper articles covering the Borden murders, trial, and aftermath. There were at least forty-three reporters and sketch artists at the trial. Local and national newspapers contained stories about Lizzie Borden and the "Trial of the Century." Today, there are hundreds of articles that recount or depict the Borden murders, or theories of what might have occurred. In popular and scholarly venues there are novels, movies, documentaries, operas, theatrical performances, musicals, event re-enactments, and trial re-enactments. Media, and the agendas of those who write for them, has had a profound influence in the shaping of our understanding of the case today.

While there have been diverse approaches to this case, we must consider media and literary outlets that, without provocation, chose to craft a public image of Lizzie as a homosexual by the use of a lesbian "terministic screen" (Burke, 1966, 45).

This essay considers media representations of a homosexual Lizzie Borden as a terministic screen from which one can justify her alleged actions or her perceived guilt. When particular terministic screens are employed in an interpretive process, certain perspectives and intentions are revealed about those employing them. By defining Lizzie Borden through selected terministic screens the interpreter can potentially receive a catharsis as she/he symbolically negotiates social tensions. In other words, authors can be cleansed of emotional tensions through the use of the contextual definitions inherent in the use of particular terministic screens (Burke, 1968). How do these devices keep the Lizzie narrative alive and emergent in new historical periods?

Print media in the Borden murders displayed different terministic screens. One of those screens crafted the notion of Lizzie Borden as a lesbian and thus began the potential justification for this heinous murder. In trying to comprehend how this crime was committed, this forged representation enabled the authors to come to terms with understanding how a Victorian woman could have committed such a vicious crime. In the typical Victorian mind women were weaker than men physically and emotionally. One could not conceptualize a woman responsible for a double axe murder. Instead, in order to excuse a woman committing this murder, she would have to be a "deviant" other—one who is not a typical woman living according to Victorian mores. A homosexual woman in

Victorian New England would fit into the category as a "deviant" other. Once depicted as a "deviant" other, Lizzie Borden could be accepted as the author of the crime. In this sense, print media and literary forms helped to establish her potential lesbian nature as a contrivance from which the general population could understand her innate ability to commit the crime.

PRINT MEDIA

In the aftermath of the Borden acquittal, Lizzie and Emma tried to rebuild their lives in Fall River. Instead of living out their days in the house at 92 Second Street, Lizzie and Emma purchased a house on the hill in Fall River, a more affluent part of town. However, their lives again became speculation for town gossip when Emma moved out of the French Street house, as the *Boston Sunday Herald* reported on June 3, 1905:[1]

> Another reported cause of the disagreement was Miss Lizzie's recent infatuation for stage folk and dramatic matters. The stage was distasteful to Miss Emma's orthodox ideas and when Miss Lizzie came to entertain a whole dramatic company at midnight hours, it passed Miss Emma's limit. And right here comes in Miss Nance O'Neil, the well known actress. It appears that Miss Lizzie and Miss O'Neil are warm personal friends. The two women met at a summer resort near Lynn last year, while Miss Borden was passing the vacation period there. A mutual attraction led to the cementing of a close and hearty friendship.

Two days after Lizzie's death, on June 3, 1927, *The Evening Standard* reported:

> Nurses who knew Miss Borden as a patient at Truesdale hospital two years ago mentioned to their friends, it is said, that she was a woman of decided opinions and will, more masculine in appearance and ways than feminine.

---

[1] All newspaper references are taken from Kent, D. (1992). *The Lizzie Borden sourcebook.* Boston: Branden Publishing Company, Inc.

On this same date the *New York Times* reported:

> Lizzie is queer,[2] but as for her being guilty I say 'no' and decidedly "no"...In 1905 Emma Borden left her sister and made her home with friends, the action causing an estrangement between the sisters.

It is evident by these messages in print media that Lizzie Borden stood out from other women in her time. Lizzie was different from most other women because she dared to speak her mind, which is one of the main reasons she was charged with the murders in the first place. It was her statement to investigating officials that caused them to question Lizzie's relationship with her stepmother, Abby. When asked if she knew who killed her father and her mother [Abby], Lizzie responded, "Mrs. Borden was not my mother; she was my stepmother. My mother died when I was a little girl" (Masterton, 16). In the Victorian era, this statement would not be seen as an appropriate response—it sounds disrespectful toward the stepmother at a time when the utterer should be more concerned with the gruesome death rather than how her relationship with the deceased is perceived.

These print media accounts were not the only references to Lizzie as a lesbian. Two contemporary novels describing fictional accounts of the Borden murders offer a similar depiction of Lizzie as a woman outside of the Victorian era norm. Elizabeth Engstrom's story may have been influenced by print media implications, while Evan Hunter's novel of the case can be seen as a representation of patriarchal values in his depiction of the crimes as sexually motivated.

NOVELS

In Elizabeth Engstrom's novel, *Lizzie Borden* (1991), the evolution of the title character as a lesbian is developed. The main focus of the story is Lizzie's infatuation with a woman named Beatrice she supposedly met

---

[2] The intended meaning of the word "queer" is to be understood as the meaning consistent with the historical moment of the Victorian era. In this sense, "queer" is not to be connoted as homosexual, rather, more likely as "different" or "odd."

while abroad on vacation. This relationship grew more intimate through correspondence between the two women, as Engstrom portrays Lizzie as being ever more infatuated with Beatrice. Her first meeting sounds more like love at first sight:

> And then she felt a presence at her side, a peachy presence, and Lizzie looked up into the world's deepest brown eyes, and the woman asked Lizzie to join her for a refreshment in the salon. Lizzie had flushed a deep crimson, she still felt the blush when she remembered. The woman must have seen or sensed her staring. She looked at the litter at her feet as if it didn't belong to her and her group and accepted the invitation...She felt so terribly inadequate and was quite puzzled that a woman such as this would spend a moment of her time with an American... (Engstrom, 1991, pp. 14-15)

Throughout their period of correspondence, Lizzie demonstrates excitement and anticipation for her newfound friend's letters. Beatrice sends Lizzie a book that she cherished and read daily. Engstrom titled the book *Pathways*. The book contained a step-by-step program for *self-discipline*. Later, however, as the novel moves forward, Lizzie has interesting experiences, similar to astral travel, which is the key to how Engstrom depicts Lizzie as the killer. Besides this aspect of *modus operandi*, Engstrom's book portrays Lizzie's relationship with Beatrice as "odd" and a "little dangerous" (37).

Elizabeth Engstrom also provides a rationale for how Lizzie Borden's name came to change to Lizbeth Borden after her acquittal— Beatrice refers to Lizzie in this way in her correspondence. Lizzie notices the name change and thinks it different, daring, and wonderful. Lizzie secretly wishes "she could be a Lizbeth in true life, and not a Lizzie" (50). While Engstrom's novel does not explicitly portray Lizzie in a physical relationship with Beatrice, Lizzie does have sexual encounters with other women in Fall River—Kathryn and Enid, Mr. Borden's mistresses. Lizzie's personality splits when she goes to her now-famous visit to the barn on the morning of the murders. It is the "bad" Lizzie who commits the crimes—the murder of Abby occurs as Lizzie masturbates; during the murder of Andrew, Lizzie eats a pear.

Evan Hunter's *Lizzie* (1984) also presents Lizzie as meeting a lady she is attracted to while abroad on her 19-week tour of Europe in 1890. This time, Lizzie and her paramour consummate the sexual act, which Hunter erotically describes as liberating Lizzie from her puritanical upbringing. After Lizzie's return home to dreary Fall River, she finds herself longing for her lover, turning instead to the maid Bridget for lesbian solace. It is this relationship that is discovered on August 4th by Abby, thereby causing Lizzie to react with rage at the intrusion into her privacy—she grabs a candlestick and bludgeons Abby to death.

In a 2002 interview published on LizzieAndrewBorden.com, Hunter explains his idea originated from news pieces that framed the reason for Emma's leaving Lizzie in 1905 as connected to Lizzie's interest in the theatre and her friendship with Nance O'Neil (i.e., lesbian actress):

> My theory was based on news articles about Lizzie's sister leaving the house, never to return, never to see Lizzie again, after an argument following the 'midnight entertainment of Lizzie's close friend, the actress Nance O'Neill.' Her sister said in a later interview, 'The happenings at the French Street house that caused me to leave, I must refuse to talk about.' And the Reverend A. E. Buck advised her that 'it was imperative' that she should 'make her home elsewhere.' Emma remarked, 'I do not expect ever to set foot on the place while she lives.' I don't know what all of that may suggest to anyone else, but I do know what it suggested to me.

In his fictional account, Hunter uses the murdering of Abby, in all its ferocity, as a true act of emancipation for Lizzie. It is in retaliation for Abby calling her "monster" and "unnatural *thing!*" that Lizzie swings the killing blows.

> She immediately rejected this deformed image of herself, blind anger rising to dispel it, suffocating rage surfacing to encompass and engulf the hopelessness of her secret passion, the chance discovery by this woman who stood quaking now against the closed door to the guest room, the fearsome threat of revelation to her father, the unfair-

ness and stupidity of not being allowed to live her own
life as she *chose* to live it!

Hunter's patriarchal value system portrays Lizzie's lesbianism as enabling
her to kill, as a violent expression of a right afforded her by her sexual
orientation. This depiction of the dangerous lesbian, the "deviant" who
acts out her rage against an unjust society, serves as an iconic other, the
woman as driven by her lesbian desire. Hunter represents that desire as
ultimately murderous and freakish, and compels us to feel the same as
we experience Lizzie's first-person lens.

Other Media Documentation

Multiple other print media outlets addressed the issue of Lizzie and
Emma's estrangement and the relationship between Nance O'Neil and
Lizzie.[3] Nance O'Neil was a stage actress whom Lizzie befriended after
her acquittal of the double murders. In the Victorian era, actors were
considered more akin to prostitutes rather than artists as we see them
today. Lizzie and Nance maintained a friendship and Nance visited Lizzie
in Fall River, while Lizzie also attended many of Nance's performances.
In fact, it was reported in several newspapers that Lizzie planned on
writing a play, based upon her own experiences, for her friend, Nance.

On June 10, 1927, the *New Bedford Standard* covered a story
specific to Lizzie and Nance O'Neil, nine days after Lizzie's death. In
this report Nance describes her relationship with Lizzie:

> When Miss O'Neil played in Boston in 1904 her person-
> ality and emotional power so gripped Miss Borden that
> she stepped out of the bonds of her habitual reserve and
> sought the acquaintance of the actress...They became
> friends and remained friends, though only in memory,
> for they never met again after Miss O'Neil finished her
> season in the East and went on a tour...No letters were
> exchanged in the nearly quarter of a century which has

---

[3] While this is not an exhaustive list, there are examples of other reports that surfaced in print
media in the aftermath of Lizzie's acquittal. For a comprehensive list of print media sources, see
Len Rebello's book, *Lizzie past & present* (Rebello, 311).

elapsed since Miss Borden and Miss O'Neil bade each other good-by. 'I am afraid I am a rather poor correspondent...We were like ships that pass in the night and speak each other in passing' (Kent, 345–346).

This interview and reporter's perspective indicates that the friendship between Lizzie and Nance was short-lived. But from this relationship the speculation of Lizzie's homosexuality was crafted.

Different print sources identified Lizzie as a potential lesbian. In the *Alyson Almanac: A Treasury of Information for the Gay and Lesbian Community*, Lizzie is listed as a "suspected homosexual" (Rebello, 431). David Salvaggio suggested:

> Lizzie Borden was a miserable and lonely lesbian, tangled in the Victorian web of the late nineteenth century; caught in a man's world long before women's suffrage. A kleptomaniac obsessed with materialism, she could no longer bear the frugal father who thwarted the lavish life she desired. And what would her future be if the bulk of the estate went to Abby?

There are multiple documentary films that provide historical record, official interviews, and, of course, potential conclusions of innocence or guilt. For example, *Evening Magazine* included Lizzie's case in a segment titled *New England Rediscovered*; the *Discovery Channel* aired a documentary on Lizzie Borden in September 1994 titled, *Lizzie Borden Took an Axe?*; Greystone Communications produced a documentary titled, *Lizzie Borden: A Woman Accused;* and the History Channel re-released *The Strange Case of Lizzie Borden* in 2005 (Bernanke). While there are many other references to Lizzie Borden that have been viewed in the documentary film industry, these are perhaps some of the obvious representations of our preoccupation with this case. In most of the documentaries, the theory of Lizzie as a lesbian is explored.

There are other theories that tantalize interest in the Borden puzzle. Rebello provides a comprehensive reference list of conspiracy theories. The only perpetrator of such an offense would still be described as a "deviant" other. The Providence *Daily Journal* posited that Lizzie conspired with another person in the act (Rebello, 123); the Boston *Daily Globe* reported that a "Frenchman" did it (Rebello, 132). Other theories suggest Dr. Bowen, the family doctor, murdered the Bordens, or Lizzie and Bridget performed the murders (136–137), or that Lizzie committed the act because of an incestuous relationship with her father (140). Another suggested Lizzie killed her parents because Andrew Borden had a love affair outside of his marriage to Abby (373) while yet another provoking theory includes conspiracy within the government itself (136).

There are definite opponents to the perspective that Lizzie murdered her father and stepmother because of a lesbian relationship or simply because she was a lesbian. In 1973 the *Fall River Herald News* reported on a lecture at the Somerset Lions Club in Somerset, Massachusetts by Dr. Jordan Fiore. In that lecture, Dr. Fiore, a resident of Taunton, Massachusetts, and a Professor of History at Bridgewater State College, negated the notion of Lizzie as a lesbian, the incest theory, and the idea that she was in the nude when she committed the act. Dr. Fiore suggested if he was a member of the jury he would have found her not guilty too, implying that there was no evidence offered to prove her guilt (Rebello, 387). While multiple theories abound, the fact is that they are theories created in the imagination of their authors who seek to comprehend an incomprehensible situation. In this case, one might ask one's self, how could this happen to a "normal" person or family? Then one might consider justifying or interpreting the circumstances through a screen that would allow a non-normal event to occur. In this case, one might use the screen of homosexuality to justify the perceived actions of Lizzie Borden as conceivable, if done by a "deviant" other.

KENNETH BURKE'S TERMINISTIC SCREENS

Kenneth Burke stated that when he speaks of terministic screens, he has particularly in mind some photographs [he] once saw. They were *different* photographs of the *same* objects, the difference being that they were made with different color filters. Here something so "factual" as a photograph revealed notable distinctions in texture, and even in form, depending upon which color filter was used for the documentary description of the event being recorded (1966, 45).

A terministic screen creates texture and shapes how one interprets the image, event, or picture. Thus, a terministic screen directs one's attention and also reveals one's intention. Therefore, consistent with the Sapir-Whorf Hypothesis (Trenholm, 272) whereby language determines thought, any set of terms that one might use to frame a description to another person acts as a terministic screen that can focus another's attention toward a particular interpretation or understanding.

Terministic screens are symbols one uses to explain to another or to interpret for one's self. These screens reveal where attention is being directed and they reveal the author's intentions at times as well. In the case of Elizabeth Engstrom, her book *Lizzie Borden* intends to explain or justify why and how Lizzie could have committed the act of parricide. Engstrom herself reveals this in her note to the reader, "My purpose is not to offend; it is to justify" (front matter). In this sense, Engstrom achieves catharsis (Burke, 1968), a way of coming to terms with the inconceivable act of parricide aggravated within a Victorian mindset.

Kenneth Burke (1966) argued that "we *must* use terministic screens, since we can't say anything without the use of terms; whatever we use, they necessarily constitute a corresponding kind of screen; and any such screen necessarily directs attention to one field [one way of seeing] rather than another" (50). It is natural to use terministic screens because human beings are symbol-using animals.

Whether Lizzie Borden was homosexual or not, we are always looking for perfection in our interpretive mode. If not careful, this perfected interpretive approach may lead to answers "rotten" with perfection (Burke, 1966, 18). To be rotten with perfection refers to a dangerous and ironic interpretive insight. To be rotten with perfection, according to Burke (1966), is dangerous because meaning is derived from connotations that could be misleading or that could misdirect our pursuit of truth(s). So, while it is admirable to pursue interpretive consummation we can also become rotten with perfection in the ironic sense if we have gone too far. It would be erroneous to conclude there has been a complete examination of Lizzie Borden's circumstances to a perfection without seeking all potential truths. Terministic screens help to pave the way toward that perfection, while understanding one must still keep a critical eye on the influence of these terministic screens to the construction of meaning.

Each message printed in a newspaper, each literary work that speculates regarding Lizzie's sexual orientation, each documentary that reports and potentially advocates Lizzie's sexuality as a justification or a scapegoat for the murders is a terministic screen that focuses the reader on that particular perspective and leads one step further toward perfection. Even though today homosexuality is more readily becoming mainstream in our Western culture compared to the status of homosexuality in the Victorian era, we still seem preoccupied with justifying, excusing, or understanding Lizzie's potential guilt through a lens that makes her different from other women—or women of the norm. Lizzie was acquitted of the charge of murder for her father, Andrew, and stepmother, Abby. This essay does not speculate on Lizzie's guilt or innocence. This statement does suggest that others who want to find Lizzie guilty might feel they need to justify her guilt by portraying her as capable of committing crime. In this case, her ethos is crafted outside of the category of "normal" and she is reconstructed as being "deviant" for her time. It is through the label of homosexual or lesbian that media crafts our image of the accused and the crime. Burke might argue that we see all reality through terministic screens and we must learn to be critical of those screens so that we see all of the intertextuality to aid our interpretation. Burke (1954/1984) suggested that our communicative efforts are imperfect because as human beings we use recalcitrant and mystifying symbols that often cause problems inherent in the act of interpretation. Whether we need to justify in our mind how a woman could have killed her parents or whether we want to capitalize on the gruesome story that will make a successful theatre production or film, we still need to consider looking for the truth and the truths connected to this case. Rhetorical inquiry will enable clearer interpretation of the circumstances.

What does it matter that Lizzie was a homosexual, if she was? What does it matter that after the murders and after her acquittal, she engaged in a lesbian relationship with one woman or multiple women? Why does her sexual orientation matter at all? Could it be that Lizzie's sexual orientation is an issue for those who remain fixated in her or his own biases while struggling to understand the act? The terministic screen of homosexuality and Lizzie's possible lesbianism might guide the author of the theory through an individual catharsis potentially "rotten" (Burke,

1961/1970) with perfection. Through this rhetorical form of keeping the Lizzie Borden mystery unsolved the story is kept alive to be considered through terministic screen after screen. In this rhetorical form we anticipate meaning as our appetite for the story increases. As our appetite builds we seek to satisfy it. The notion of Lizzie Borden as a lesbian satisfies an appetite, creates a catharsis, and helps us to make sense out of the incomprehensible.

Recognizing the rhetoric of Lizzie's homosexuality portrayed through media as a terministic screen provides a distance necessary for understanding and explanation because it reminds us not to become a victim of mere persuasion, or worse, manipulation.

We have attempted to introduce Lizzie Borden to the reader through an account of the circumstances involved in this particular case and demonstrate that multiple media outlets portray Lizzie Borden as a lesbian, or implied the potential for Lizzie to be homosexual. In this case, an understanding of the function of terministic screens, the sociocultural space of women in the Victorian era, and the role of media outlets then and now, suggests that in trying to justify *why* Lizzie committed this act, opponents of Lizzie's innocence redefine her as a "deviant" in society. Thus they create her ethos through a terministic screen of homosexuality, which is not so much evidence of her "guilt" as a lesbian woman, but rather it is evidence of the author's conceptualization of who can commit such a "deviant" act.

REFERENCES

Arnett, R.C. & Arneson, P. (1999). *Dialogic civility in a cynical age: Community, hope, and interpersonal relationships.* New York: SUNY Press.

Bernanke, J. (Producer). (2005). *History's mysteries: The strange case of Lizzie Borden* [DVD]. United States; Canada: A&E Television.

Burke, K. (1954/1984). *Permanence and change: An anatomy of purpose.* Berkeley: University of California Press.

Burke, K. (1961/1970). *Rhetoric of religion: Studies in logology.* Berkeley: University of California Press.

Burke, K. (1966). *Language as symbolic action: Essays on life, literature, and method.* Los Angeles: University of California Press.

Burke, K. (1968). *Counterstatement.* Berkeley: University of California Press.

Burke, K. (1969). *A Grammar of motives.* Los Angeles: University of California Press.

Engstrom, E. (1991). *Lizzie Borden.* New York: Tom Doherty Associates.

Holba, A. (2003). Shattering the myth: A Burkean analysis of motive and myth. *Lizzie Borden Quarterly. 10*(3), 10–18.

Holba, A. (2004). The rhetoric of gender bias in Victorian New England: An ongoing dialectic. *The Hatchet: Journal of Lizzie Borden Studies.* (1)1.

Hyde, M. J. (in press). *Searching for perfection: Martin Heidegger (with some help from Kenneth Burke) on language, truth, and the practice of rhetoric.* In P. Arneson (Ed.) *Perspectives of Philosophy of Communication.* West Lafayette, IN: Purdue University Press.

Kent, D. (1992). *Lizzie Borden sourcebook.* Boston: Branden Publishing Company, Inc.

Lyne, J. (1998). *Philosophical approaches to communication theory. Journal of Communication. 48*(3) 153–158.

Lyotard, J. F. (1984). *The postmodern condition: A report on knowledge: Theory and history of literature.* Minneapolis, MN: University of Minnesota Press.

Masterson, W. (2000). *Lizzie didn't do it*. Boston: Branden Publishing Company, Inc.

Rebello, L. (1999). *Lizzie Borden past & present: A comprehensive reference to the life and times of Lizzie Borden*. Fall River, MA: Al-Zach Press.

Salvaggio, D. W. (1994). Whodunit?: A Borden buff's theory on the crime. *Lizzie Borden Quarterly*. 2(2), p. 6.

Schrag, C.O. (2003). *Communicative praxis and the space of subjectivity*. West Lafayette, IN: Purdue University Press.

Stewart, J. (1995). *Language as articulate contact: Toward a post-semiotic philosophy of communication*. New York: SUNY Press.

Questions for Discussion
on Chapter 7

1. Identify several reasons why the case of Lizzie Borden maintains significant interest in American scholarly and popular culture.
2. Define Kenneth Burke's terministic screens. How do they function in our interpretive actions?
3. Can you think of another historical case in popular culture consciousness that has similar continued interest? If so, what do you suppose are reasons for this continued interest?
4. Can you identify points of similarity between the case of Lizzie Borden and the case of O.J. Simpson?

CHAPTER 8

CONCLUSION

This text used an infamous criminal case that has permeated the popular culture consciousness, in at least the Northeastern United States, to explore the application of selected theoretical frameworks that include works from Marcus Cicero, Kenneth Burke, Hans-Georg Gadamer, Paul Ricoeur, and Walter Fisher. Through these theoretical frameworks we can learn to hone our critical thinking skills and teach us how to engage persuasive mediated artifacts as competent communicators. This text is not meant to be a comprehensive examination of all communication theories but instead it is meant to take selected theories and explore how they work within real world contexts and enable us to weed through fallacies of judgment and basic persuasive attacks upon our reasoning. The case of Lizzie Borden seemed particularly useful as an example because of the plethora of artifacts available for examination. This text is meant to demonstrate how communication theories inform our critical thinking skills and our communication competence so that we can understand communicative actions at deeper levels. This deeper understanding permits us to unite theory and practice for a richer praxial understanding of human communicative engagement.

Whether considering forensic aspects of events from a Ciceronian perspective, the search for motives using a Burkean framework, a phenomenological consideration of time and space through the philosophies of Gadamer or Ricoeur, or the import of narrative theory from Fisher and

Roberts, we can learn so much more about human communication, related consequences, and tangential encounters if we have an idea of where to begin our reflections. These selected theories are starting places that help us to understand theories and application in specific contexts. It is the hope of this text that by using the case of Lizzie Borden the value of understanding communication theory related to the human experience will be illuminated. It is also another hope that we can use other popular culture artifacts, regardless of where they fall in historical time periods, to help us gain insight and comprehension into the nature of human experience and to the particular actions we try so hard to understand. It is my hope that this approach resonates with you, the reader, as rhetorical agents yourselves.

BIBLIOGRAPHY

Aristotle. (1984). *The rhetoric and poetics*. New York: Modern Library College Edition.

Arnett, R.C. & Arneson, P. (1999). *Dialogic civility in a cynical age: Community, hope, and interpersonal relationships*. New York: SUNY Press.

Belknap, J. (2001). *The invisible woman: Gender, crime, and justice*. Belmont, CA: Wadsworth.

Bernanke, J. (Producer). (2005). *History's mysteries: The strange case of Lizzie Borden* [Television documentary]. United States; Canada: A&E Television.

Bitzer, L. F. (1968). The rhetorical situation. *Philosophy and Rhetoric*. 1, 1–14.

Brown, A. (1991). *Lizzie Borden: The legend, the truth, the final chapter*. Nashville, TN: Rutledge Hill Press.

Bryant, D. C. (1953). Rhetoric: Its function and scope. *Quarterly Journal of Speech*. 39, 401–424.

Burgchardt, C. R. (Ed.) *Readings in rhetorical criticism*. State College, PA: Strata Publishing.

Burke, K. (1973). *The philosophy of literary form*. Berkeley: University of California Press.

Burke, K. (1970). *The rhetoric of religion*. Berkeley: University of California Press.

Burke, K. (1969). *A grammar of motives*. Los Angeles: University of California Press.

Burke, K. (1968). *Counter-statement*. Berkeley: University of California Press.

Burke, K. (1966). *Language as symbolic action: Essays on life, literature, and method*. Los Angeles: University of California Press.

Burke, K. (1964). *Perspectives by incongruity*. Bloomington, IN: Indiana University Press.

Burke, K. (1961/1970). *Rhetoric of religion: Studies in logology*. Berkeley: University of California Press.

Burke, K. (1955). *A rhetoric of motives*. New York: Braziller, Inc.

Burke, K. (1954/1984). *Permanence and change: An anatomy of purpose*. Berkeley: University of California Press.

DeMille, A. (1968). *Lizzie Borden: A dance of death*. Boston: Little Brown and Co.

DeVito, J. A. (2004). *The interpersonal communication book*. Boston: Allyn and Bacon.

Ehninger, D. (1968). On the systems of rhetoric. *Philosophy and Rhetoric*. 1, 131–144.

Ellul, J. (1985). *The humiliation of the word*. Grand Rapids, MI: William B. Eerdmans Publishing.

Engstrom, E. (1991). *Lizzie Borden*. New York: Tom Doherty Associates.

Fisher, W. (1989). *Human communication as narration: Toward a philosophy of reason, value, and action*. Columbia, SC: University of South Carolina Press.

Flynn, R. (1985). Foreword. In Edwin Porter, *The Fall River tragedy: A history of the Borden murders*. Portland, ME: King Phillip Publishing Co.

Gadamer, H. G. (2002). *Truth and method*. New York: Continuum.

Gustafson, A. (1985). *Guilty or innocent?* New York: Holt, Rinehart, Winston.

Hart, R. (1990). *Modern rhetorical criticism*. Glenville, IL: Scott Foresman.

Herrick, J.A. (2005). *The history and theory of rhetoric: An introduction*. Boston: Allyn and Bacon.

History's Mysteries: The strange case of Lizzie Borden. (1996). A&E Television Networks. New York: New Video Group.

Holba, A. (2007a) Abby Durfee Gray Borden: Representation of an archetypal wicked stepmother. In Kylo Hart. (Ed.). *Media(ted) deviance and social otherness: Interrogating influential representations.* Cambridge: Cambridge Scholar's Press.

Holba, A. (2007b). *Philosophical leisure: Recuperative praxis for human communication.* Milwaukee, WI: Marquette University Press.

Holba, A. (2007c). Lizzie as "deviant" other: Interpretation of otherness. *The Hatchet: Journal of Lizzie Borden Studies.* 4(2), 6–13.

Holba, A. (2005). Edwin Porter's *The Fall River tragedy:* A hermeneutic entrance into the Borden mystery. *The Hatchet: Journal of Lizzie Borden Studies.* 2(6), 6–12.

Holba, A. (2005). The trial testimony of John V. Morse. *The Hatchet: Journal of Lizzie Borden Studies.* 2(5), 6–13.

Holba, A. (2004). The rhetoric of gender bias in Victorian New England: An ongoing dialectic. *The Hatchet: Journal of Lizzie Borden Studies.* (1)1.

Holba, A. (2003). Shattering the myth: A Burkean analysis of motive and myth. *Lizzie Borden Quarterly.* 10(3), 10–18.

Hunter, E. (1984). *Lizzie.* New York: Arbor House.

Hyde, M. J. (2007). *Searching for perfection: Martin Heidegger (with some help from Kenneth Burke) on language, truth, and the practice of rhetoric.* In P. Arneson (Ed.) *Perspectives of philosophy of communication.* West Lafayette, IN: Purdue University Press.

Hyde, M. (2006). *Life-giving gift of acknowledgment.* West Lafayette, IN: Purdue University Press.

Isocrates. (1928/1945). *Isocrates.* 3 vols. Trans. George Norlin (vol. 1–2) and LaRue VanHook (vol. 3). London: William Heinemann.

Kent, D. (1992a). *Lizzie Borden sourcebook.* Boston: Branden Publishing Company, Inc.

Kent, D. (1992b). *Forty whacks: New evidence in the life and legend of Lizzie Borden.* Emmanus, PA: Yankee Books.

Kronenwetter, M. (1967). *Free press v. fair trial.* New York: Franklin Watts.

Lincoln, V. (1967). *A private disgrace: Lizzie Borden by daylight.* New York: G.P. Putnam's and Sons.

Lustgarten, E. (1950). *Verdict in dispute.* New York: Charles Scribner and Sons.

Lyne, J. (1998). Philosophical approaches to communication theory. *Journal of Communication. 48*(3) 153–158.

Lyotard, J. F. (1984). *The postmodern condition: A report on knowledge: Theory and history of literature.* Minneapolis, MN: University of Minnesota Press.

Masterson, W. (2000). *Lizzie didn't do it.* Boston: Branden Publishing Company, Inc.

Meyer, J. (1996). Seeking organizational unity: Building bridges in response to mystery. *Southern Communication Journal. 61*(3), 210–220.

Muraskin, R. (2001). *It's a crime: Woman and justice.* Upper Saddle River, NJ: Prentice Hall.

Porter, E. (1985/1893). *The Fall River tragedy: A history of the Borden murders.* Portland, ME: King Phillip Publishing.

Poulakos, T. *Speaking for the polis: Isocrates rhetorical education.* Columbia, SC: University of South Carolina Press.

Radin, E. (1961). *Lizzie Borden: The untold story.* New York: Simon and Schuster.

Rappaport, D. (1992). *Lizzie Borden: Be the judge, be the jury.* New York: Harper-Collins.

Rebello, L. (1999). *Lizzie Borden past & present: A comprehensive reference to the life and times of Lizzie Borden.* Fall River, MA: Al-Zach Press.

Ricoeur, P. (1988). *Time and narrative.* vol. 3. Chicago: University of Chicago Press.

Roberts, K.G. (2004). Texturing the narrative paradigm: Folklore and communication. *Communication Quarterly. 52*(2), 129–142.

Rorty, R. (1979). *Philosophy and the mirror of nature.* Princeton, NJ: Princeton University Press.

Salibrici, M. (1999). Dissonance and rhetorical inquiry: A Burkean model for critical reading and writing. *Journal of Adolescent and Adult Literacy. 42*(8), 628–637.

Salvaggio, D. W. (1994). Whodunit?: A Borden buff's theory on the crime. *Lizzie Borden Quarterly. 2*(2), p. 6.

Satterthwait, W. (1989). *Miss Lizzie.* New York: St. Martin's Press.

Schrag, C.O. (2003). *Communicative praxis and the space of subjectivity.* West Lafayette, IN: Purdue University Press.

Shanley, M. (1989). *Feminism, marriage, and the law in Victorian New England.* Princeton, NJ: Princeton University Press.

Showalter, E. (1997). *Hystories.* New York: Columbia University Press.

Spiering, F. (1984). *Lizzie.* New York: Random House.

Stewart, J. (1995). *Language as articulate contact: Toward a post-semiotic philosophy of communication.* New York: SUNY Press.

Sullivan, R. (1974). *Goodbye Lizzie Borden.* Brattleboro, VT: Stephen Greene Press.

Swartz, O. (1996). Kenneth Burke's theory of form: Rhetoric, art, and cultural analysis. *Southern Communication Journal. 61*(4), 312–322.

Weaver, R.M. (1970). *Language is sermonic: Richard M. Weaver on the nature of rhetoric.* Baton Rouge, LA: Louisiana State University Press.

Williams, J.G., Smithburn, J.E., Peterson, M.J. (Eds.) (1980). *Lizzie Borden: A case book of family and crime in the 1890s.* Bloomington, IN: T.I.S. Publishing.

Wood, J. (2006). *Gendered lives: Communication, gender, and culture.* Belmont, CA: Wadsworth.

LIZZIE BORDEN BIBLIOGRAPHY

**A comprehensive Lizzie Borden Bibliography can be accessed in Leonard Rebello's 1999 comprehensive work entitled, *Lizzie Borden Past & Present: A Comprehensive Reference to the Life and Times of Lizzie Borden.*

The following bibliography is a compendium containing many of the significant works about the case of Lizzie Borden. This list is not limited to books. A comprehensive periodical bibliography is available also in Rebello's book, *Lizzie Borden Past & Present.* The list below is designed to be a resource that will aid any Lizzie enthusiast in pursuit of research into the case of Lizzie Borden through a critical eye and a rhetorical inquiry.

Adler, G. S. (1995). *Our beloved Lizzie: Constructing an American legend.* Kingston, RI: University of Rhode Island. [Dissertation].

Bernanke, J. (Producer). (1999). *History's mysteries: The strange case of Lizzie Borden* [Television documentary]. United States; Canada: A&E Television.

Boar, R., & Blundell, N. (1984). *The world's most infamous murders.* New York: Exeter Books.

Boss, J. (1982). *Fall River: A pictorial history*. Norfolk, VA: Donning Co. Pub.

Brown, A. (1991). *Lizzie Borden: The legend, the truth, the final chapter*. Nashville, TN: Rutledge Hill Press.

Callahan, S. (1994). *Forty whacks*. New York: St. Martin's Press.

Canning, J. (1987). *Unsolved murders and mysteries*. Secaucus, NJ: Chartwell Books.

Churchill, A. (1964). *A pictorial history of American crime: 1829-1929*. New York: Holt, Reinhart & Winston.

Davenport, S. M. (1992). *Miss Lizzie A. Borden paperdolls and Victorian pastimes*. Fall River: Fall River Historical Society

DeMille, A. (1968). *Lizzie Borden: A dance of death*. Boston: Little Brown and Co.

Dunbar, D. (1964). *Blood in the parlor*. New York: A. S. Barnes & Co.

Engstrom, E. (1991). *Lizzie Borden*. New York: Tom Doherty Associates.

Flynn, R. (1985). Foreword. In Edwin Porter, *The Fall River tragedy: A history of the Borden murders*. Portland, ME: King Phillip Publishing Co.

Flynn, R. (1992a). *The Borden murders: An annotated bibliography*. Portland, ME: King Phillip Publishing.

Flynn, R. (1992b). *Lizzie Borden and the mysterious axe*. Portland, ME: King Phillip Publishing.

Gustafson, A. (1985). *Guilty or innocent?* New York: Holt, Rinehart, Winston.

Haskell, O. (1993). *Lizzie!*. (play)

Haskell, O. (1997). *Sherlock Holmes and the Fall River tragedy*. North Providence, RI: Lazarus Press.

Holba, A. (2007a) Abby Durfee Gray Borden: Representation of an archetypal wicked stepmother. In Kylo Hart. (Ed.). *Media(ted) deviance and social otherness: Interrogating influential representations*. Cambridge: Cambridge Scholar's Press.

Holba, A. (2007c). Lizzie as "deviant" other: Interpretation of otherness. *The Hatchet: Journal of Lizzie Borden Studies*. 4(2), 6–13.

Holba, A. (2005). Edwin Porter's *The Fall River tragedy*: A hermeneutic entrance into the Borden mystery. *The Hatchet: Journal of Lizzie Borden Studies. 2*(6), 6–12.

Holba, A. (2005). The trial testimony of John V. Morse. *The Hatchet: Journal of Lizzie Borden Studies. 2*(5), 6–13.

Holba, A. (2004). The rhetoric of gender bias in Victorian New England: An ongoing dialectic. *Journal of Lizzie Borden Studies.* (1)1.

Holba, A. (2003). Shattering the myth: A Burkean analysis of motive and myth. *Lizzie Borden Quarterly. 10*(3), 10–18.

Hunter, E. (1984). *Lizzie*. New York: Arbor House.

Kent, D. (1991). *Slaughter on Second Street*. Shreveport, LA: Rosebud Productions. (play)

Kent, D. (1992a). *Lizzie Borden sourcebook*. Boston: Branden Publishing Company, Inc.

Kent, D. (1992b). *Forty whacks: New evidence in the life and legend of Lizzie Borden*. Emmanus, PA: Yankee Books.

Kronenwetter, M. (1967). *Free press v. fair trial*. New York: Franklin Watts.

Lawrence, R. (1959). *The legend of Lizzie*. Chicago: Dramatic Club Pub. (play)

Lincoln, V. (1967). *A private disgrace: Lizzie Borden by Daylight*. New York: G.P. Putnam's and Sons.

Lizzie Borden: Did she or didn't she? (1992). Verplanck, NY: Historical Briefs.

Lowndes, M. B. (1939). *Lizzie Borden: A study in conjecture*. New York: Longman.

Lunday, T. (1893). *Mystery unveiled: The truth about the Borden tragedy*. Providence, RI: J.A. & R.A. Reid.

Lustgarten, E. (1950). *Verdict in dispute*. New York: Charles Scribner and Sons.

Marshall, J. D. (1990). *Lizzie Borden and the library connection*. Tallahassee, FL: School of Library & Information, FSU.

Martins, M., & Binette, D. (1994). *The Commonwealth of Massachusetts vs. Lizzie A. Borden: The Knowlton papers, 1892-1893*. Fall River, MA: Fall River Historical Society.

Masterson, W. (2000). *Lizzie didn't do it.* Boston: Branden Publishing Company, Inc.

Pearson, E. L. (1937). *The trial of Lizzie Borden.* Garden City, NY: Doubleday.

Porter, E. (1893). *The Fall River tragedy: A history of the Borden murders.* Portland, ME: King Phillip Publishing.

Radin, E. (1961). *Lizzie Borden: The untold story.* New York: Simon and Schuster.

Rappaport, D. (1992). *Lizzie Borden: Be the judge, be the jury.* New York: Harper-Collins.

Rebello, L. (1999). *Lizzie Borden past & present: A comprehensive reference of the life and times of Lizzie Borden.* Fall River, MA: Al-Zach Press.

Salvaggio, D. W. (1994). Whodunit?: A Borden buff's theory on the crime. *Lizzie Borden Quarterly. 2*(2), p. 6.

Sams, E. (1992). *Lizzie Borden unlocked.* Ben Lamond, CA: Yellow Tulip Press.

Satterthwait, W. (1989). *Miss Lizzie.* New York: St. Martin's Press.

Songini, M. (1995). *New England's most sensational murders.* Attleboro, MA: Covered Bridge Press.

Spiering, F. (1984). *Lizzie.* New York: Random House.

Sullivan, R. (1974). *Goodbye Lizzie Borden.* Brattleboro, VT: Stephen Greene Press.

Whitman, R. (1973). *The passion of Lizzie Borden.* New York: October House.

Williams, J.G., Smithburn, J.E., Peterson, M.J. (Eds.) (1980). *Lizzie Borden: A case book of family and crime in the 1890s.* Bloomington, IN: T.I.S. Publishing.

INDEX

A

Aristotle, 75, 106

Arneson, P., 107, 118, 121, 124, 138, 152

Arnett, R.C., 107, 118, 121, 124, 138, 152

B

Bence, Eli, 5, 63

Blaisdell, Josiah (Hon.), 4, 5, 21, 30, 48, 50, 77, 90

Borden, Abby Durfee Gray, 2–3, 6, 8–10, 43–44, 60, 86, 93, 95–96, 102, 107, 110, 112, 114, 122, 127–128, 131, 139, 143–145, 147–148, 150

Borden, Andrew Jackson, 1–3, 6–9, 15, 37, 43, 52, 59, 61–62, 95–96, 107, 110–112, 128, 131, 148

Borden, Emma Lenora, 2–3, 6–7, 18, 53–54, 62, 71, 107, 110, 127, 130–131, 142–143, 145–146

Borden, Lizbeth, 69–74, 144

Borden, Sarah Morse, 2–3

Bowen, Seabury (Dr.), 4–5, 8, 21, 62, 78, 92–93, 99–100, 132, 148

Burke, K., 10, 13–17, 19–20, 31, 33–40, 69–70, 73–75, 141, 148–150, 152, 154–155

C

catharsis, 35, 70, 72–74, 141, 149–151

Churchill, Adelaide, 5, 8, 93, 99–101

Cicero, M.T., 104–106, 118–119, 155

D

deviant, 140–142, 146–148, 150–151

Dolan, William (Dr.), 4, 95–97, 115

dramatism, 13

E

Ellul, J., 70–71, 75–76

emplotment, 1, 107

CPSIA information can be obtained
at www.ICGtesting.com
Printed in the USA
FFHW010051120219
50481549-55724FF